MENTAL ILLNESS

VOLUME 1 of 5

The Necessity for Faith & Authority

by
Dr. Daniel R. Berger II

Mental Illness: The Necessity for Faith and Authority, Volume 1

Library of Congress Control Number: 2016906920
Trade Paperback ISBN: 978-0-9864114-4-1
Cover Artwork by: Elieser Loewenthal
Edited by: Laurie Buck

Copyright © 2016 by Daniel R. Berger II

All rights reserved. No part of this publication may be reproduced or transmitted in any form or by any means, electronic or mechanical, including recording, photocopying, or by any retrieval system or information storage except for brief quotations in printed reviews, without the prior written permission of the publisher, except as provided by USA copyright law.

Published by Alethia International Publications - Taylors, SC

www.drdanielberger.com

Printed in the United States of America.

To
my wonderful grandparents
Dr. Walter and Trudy Fremont.
This series of books was in many ways
made possible through their
example, support, teaching, prayer,
and love for God and others.

TABLE OF CONTENTS

INTRODUCTION	17
CHAPTER 1 – DECIDING NORMALCY	30
CHAPTER 2 – CREATING MENTAL ILLNESS	45
CHAPTER 3 – DEFINING MENTAL ILLNESS	63
CHAPTER 4 – DIAGNOSING MENTAL ILLNESS	85
CHAPTER 5 – CONTROLLING MENTAL ILLNESS	103
CHAPTER 6 – UNDERSTANDING MENTAL ILLNESS	110
CHAPTER 7 – SEEKING CAUSES OF MENTAL ILLNESS	119
CHAPTER 8 – ACCEPTING THE BIBLICAL WORLDVIEW	121
CONCLUSION	132
APPENDICES	135
BIBLIOGRAPHY	139

ACKNOWLEDGMENTS

This project was made possible by many friends, family, and professionals who sacrificed time and gave effort to read early drafts and offer me valuable feedback, conversations, and suggestions. Specifically, I would like to thank my wife, Oriana, and my parents, Dan and Gail Berger, who both patiently encouraged me through the several years of research and writing and engaged in useful discussions with me throughout the process. I wish to also thank a group of people that consists of several therapists, a neurosurgeon, a functional neurologist, pastors, a former psychiatrist, and others with medical backgrounds: Laura Beauvais, Ethan Stanley, Dr. Christina Biester, Trudy Fremont, Dr. Hugh Clarke, Tim Lovegrove, Dr. Kevin Hurt, Dr. Joe Henson, Dr. Elliot Hirshorn, Dr. Gregg Mazak, and John Hutchison, Jr. Additionally, Gayle and Marcy Broughton, James Moran, and Jeff Clemens contributed valuable insight and discussion along the way. Likewise, the hard work of my editor, Laurie Buck, has been essential to the final product. Finally, I want to thank all the individuals and families who over the past many years have allowed me to be a small part of their lives in offering them Scriptural answers that enable them to have life more abundantly and to progress in allowing God to renew their mind.

DISCLAIMER

The material contained in this book is the result of years of experience, research, professional interviews, but it is not intended in any way to be taken as medical advice. Rather, the views and material expressed in this book are philosophical and historical in nature and written in order to provide truth and hope that will enable pastors, clinicians, therapists, counselors, university professors, and other professionals to be better equipped to offer genuine truth, love, and hope to those in their care.

ABBREVIATIONS

ANS	Autonomic Nervous System
APA	American Psychiatric Association
ADHD	Attention Deficit-Hyperactivity Disorder
DSM-5	*Diagnostic & Statistical Manual of Mental Disorders 5*
ESV	*English Standard Version*
FDA	Federal Drug Administration
ICD	International Classification of Disorders
JAMA	*Journal of the American Medical Association*
KJV	*King James Version*
NAMI	National Alliance for the Mentally Ill
NEJM	*New England Journal of Medicine*
NIH	National Institutes of Health
NIMH	National Institute of Mental Health
NIV	*New International Version*
WHO	World Health Organization

BOOK SERIES

This book is one volume of five in a series on the current construct of mental illness. Each volume builds upon the other in a logical and progressive explanation. Although each volume can be read separately and out of order, following the designed order will provide the most benefit to the reader.

Volume 1 – *The Necessity for Faith and Authority*

Volume 2 – *The Reality of the Spiritual Nature*

Volume 3 – *The Reality of the Physical Nature*

Volume 4 – *The Influence of Nurture*

Volume 5 – *The Necessity for Dependence*

BOOK SERIES PREFACE

> Mental constructs of reality are imperfect, but indispensable, ways to organize the otherwise bewildering phenomena of the world.[1] – psychiatrist and chairman of the *DSM-IV* task force, Allen Frances

> The problem of mental disorder is probably as old as man. Recorded history reports a broad range of interpretations of abnormal behavior and methods for its alleviation or eradication, which have generally reflected the degree of enlightenment and the trends of religious, philosophical, and social beliefs and practices of the times.[2] – *Abnormal Psychology*

Since the 1950s, psychiatry has controlled both the definitions, theories, diagnoses, and suggested remedies for mental illness.[3] Many intelligent, well-educated, and well-meaning people have blindly accepted the secular construct of mental illness without investigating the underlying theories or answering foundational questions necessary to form a construct of mental illness. Some have chosen to refrain from conversations out of ignorance or fear of hurting and distancing themselves from friends or family who are labeled as mentally ill. Still others have taken dogmatic positions often erring on the side of ignoring truth or disregarding empathy. The time for society and especially for Christians to logically and carefully examine the current mental health system is well overdue.

---

[1] Allen Frances, *Saving Normal: An Insider's Revolt against Diagnosis, DSM-5, Big Pharma, and the Medicalization of Ordinary Life* (New York: HarperCollins, 2013), 21.

[2] Walter Coville, Timothy Costello, and Fabian Rouke, *Abnormal Psychology: Mental Illness Types, Causes, and Treatment* (New York: Barnes and Noble, 1960), 11.

[3] Specifically, those who hold to the paradigm set forth by the father of psychiatry Emil Kraepelin currently control the mental health system.

Many mental health professionals understand that the current construct and system are broken and that mental health reform must be a priority. Psychiatrist Gina Nikkel remarks,

> Since the modern version of our mental health system was initiated over 60 years ago, it has grown exponentially and has become more rigid and, ironically, far less responsive to the needs of persons labeled with psychiatric distress and their families despite all the efforts, costs, rules, regulations, and reimbursement strategies applied to reduce psychological distress.[4]

Like Dr. Nikkel, the British Psychological Society in 2013 claimed,

> There is no scientific evidence that psychiatric diagnoses such as schizophrenia and bipolar disorder are valid or useful. . . . In a groundbreaking move that has already prompted a fierce backlash from psychiatrists, the British Psychological Society's division of clinical psychology (DCP) . . . [declared] that, given the lack of evidence, it is time for a "paradigm shift" in how the issues of mental health are understood. The statement effectively casts doubt on psychiatry's predominantly biomedical model of mental distress – the idea that people are suffering from illnesses that are treatable by doctors using drugs. The DCP said its decision to speak out "reflects fundamental concerns about the development, personal impact and core assumptions of the (diagnosis) systems," used by psychiatry. Dr Lucy Johnstone, a consultant clinical psychologist who helped draw up the DCP's statement, said it was unhelpful to see mental health issues as illnesses with biological causes.[5]

Similarly, neuroscientist Elliot Valenstein asserts,

> These ideas [fundamental to the current mental health system] are simply an unproven hypothesis, but . . . they are heavily promoted as a well-substantiated explanatory theory. Because these ideas have enormous implications, there is a great need to examine the evidence and basic assumptions much more critically than has been done up to now.[6]

---

[4] Gina Nikkel, "How to Fix the Broken Mental Health System: Ten Crucial Changes," *Psychiatric Times* (November 7, 2014), http://www.psychiatrictimes.com/career/how-fix-broken-mental-health-system-ten-crucial-changes#sthash.bWF2sHtk.dpu.

[5] Jamie Doward, "Psychiatrists under Fire in Mental Health Battle," *Guardian*, (May 11, 2013), http://www.theguardian.com/society/2013/may/12/psychiatrists-under-fire-mental-health?CMP=share_btn_tw.

[6] Elliot Valenstein, *Blaming the Brain: The Truth about Drugs and Mental Health* (New York: Basic Books, 1998), 3.

The pressing need to examine what is normal and abnormal caused the chair of the American Psychiatric Association's *Diagnostic and Statistical Manual-IV (DSM-IV)*,[7] Allen Frances, to write a book called *Saving Normal*[8] in which he questions the past, present, and future of the current mental health construct. So many problems and unanswered questions now exist that a number of psychiatrists and clinical professionals claim that psychiatry and the current construct it espouses are in a major crisis, and that consensus continues to grow.[9] These sentiments represent those of many once-prominent professionals who admit that the current ideas about mental illness are not helping society advance, but rather they are turning normal into illness and, more often than not, failing to meet the needs of individuals who are struggling. Many clinicians not only realize that things must change, they are actively involved in making sure these changes come to fruition.[10]

If secular professionals are willing to question, to consider the current system as broken, and to look more critically at its existence, then certainly Christians must do the same. Since investigation and criticism of the current foundations of mental illness are clearly needed, an alternative, reliable and valid

---

[7] American Psychiatric Association, *Diagnostic and Statistical Manual of Mental Disorders: DSM-IV-TR* (Washington, DC: American Psychiatric Association, 2000).

[8] Frances, *Saving Normal*, 17.

[9] For more on this subject, see Lawrie Reznek, *Peddling Mental Disorder: The Crisis in Modern Psychiatry* (Jefferson, NC: McFarland, 2016). See also Richard Bentall, *Madness Explained: Psychosis and Human Nature* (New York: Penguin, 2003).

[10] "I believe that many psychologists and psychiatrists can sense that a new way of thinking about psychiatric disorders is emerging, but few will have had the opportunity to try to gather together the many different strands of research that are contributing to this shift in thinking" (Richard Bentall, *Madness Explained: Psychosis and Human Nature* [New York: Penguin, 2003], 111).

solution must be offered as well. Likewise, such an alternative must address the many unanswered questions that the current secular construct of mental illness has failed to supply.

If we are to repair what is clearly broken, we must be willing to examine underlying presuppositions of the current construct, to discuss sometimes taboo topics, question current positions, and accept the objective conclusions. Psychiatrist Emmanuel Stip once suggested, "If we wish to base psychiatry on evidence-based medicine, we run a genuine risk in taking a closer look at what has long been considered fact."[11] Yet, if we truly desire to help those suffering under the diagnosis of mental illness, we must be willing to question dogma and be prepared to change our minds as necessary.

Some of these dogmas are foundational to the current construct's existence and social acceptance. Two of the most prevalent underlying beliefs are 1) science is the key to understanding mental illness and 2) medicine provides the only viable remedy to mental struggles. When these propositions were created and why they must be maintained in order for the current construct of mental illness to continue its control over society are important issues that must be objectively explored. Andrew Scull remarks in his book, *Madness in Civilization*:

> Besides, the manifestations of madness, its meanings, its consequences, where one draws the boundary between sanity and insanity--then and now--these are matters that are deeply affected by the social context within which unreason surfaces and is contained. Context matters and we cannot attain an Archimedean view from nowhere, beyond the partialities of the present, from which we might survey in a neutral and unbiased fashion the complexities of history.[12]

---

[11] Emmanuel Stip, "Happy Birthday, Neuroleptics!" *European Psychiatry* 17 (2002): 115-19.

[12] Andrew Scull, *Madness in Civilization: A Cultural History of Insanity from the Bible to Freud, from the Madhouse to Modern Medicine* (Princeton, NJ: Princeton University Press 2015), 15.

The history of madness, which most secular historians focus on when discussing mental illness, is relevant, but it is a small part of the discussion. Attention must primarily be given to the underlying belief system and philosophies that guide both the perception of abnormal and the approaches to mental illness. In the process, this series of books will seek to demonstrate that faith, authority, and dependence are far more relevant issues than they may appear, and that a proper perspective of them can lead to a valid remedy more readily than can alleged science and current medical practices.

Another equally popular tenet of faith within the current mental health construct is the suggestion that religion and science are conflicting ideas. Secular authorities propose that one or the other must be accepted, and that though a religious perspective was once an accepted approach, science has now taken its place.[13] In their view, to reject their construct and claims of scientific discovery is inhumane. Yet as we will see, even prominent psychiatrists understand and admit that there exist various empathetic and alternative theories and approaches to the same problems.[14]

Throughout most of history, soul care[15] was the privilege and responsibility of people of faith and not the physician. This privilege and responsibility remains a biblical mandate—a task which many Christians willingly practice. In fact Christian

---

[13] Frances, *Saving Normal*, 35-76.

[14] Ibid., 36.

[15] The term *psychiatry* means "medical treatment of the soul" (Jeffrey A. Lieberman, *Shrinks: the Untold Story of Psychiatry* [New York: Little, Brown and Company, 2015], 27).

counseling is still practiced and flourishing.[16] However, the secular construct is not a replacement theory of caring for souls[17] but an alternative theory from a worldview contrary to the Bible.

In 1770 German-born Franz Anton Mesmer first suggested that the explanation and care for the soul should lie within a physiological framework.[18] Former president-elect of the APA Dr. Jeffery Lieberman remarks on this point of history,

> In the 1770s [Mesmer] rejected the prevailing religious and moral accounts of mental illness in favor of a physiological explanation, making him arguably the world's first psychiatrist.[19]

Like modern psychiatric theory, Mesmer's theory of "animal magnetism" was proposed and accepted on scientific claims but with faith and speculation as its reality.[20] One historian explains the power of faith involved in both theory and treatment outcomes,

> As Mesmer's fame spread, more and more people flocked to be cured by him, and even people of rank began to notice the doctor from Vienna. . . . They soon reached the conclusion that the magnetic rays were nonexistent and any beneficial result from such treatment was due to self-suggestion.[21]

---

[16] Stuart Scott and Heath Lambert, eds., *Counseling the Hard Cases: True Stories Illustrating the Sufficiency of God's Resources in Scripture* (Nashville: B&H Publishing Group, 2012).

[17] Roy Porter, *Madness a Brief History* (New York: Oxford University Press, 2002), 33.

[18] Most secularists believe that Mesmer was the first psychiatrist, though some, like Allen Frances, suggest Philippe Pinel (Frances, *Saving Normal*, 56).

[19] Jeffrey A. Lieberman, *Shrinks: the Untold Story of Psychiatry* (New York: Little, Brown and Company, 2015), 27.

[20] Joe Dispenza, *You Are the Placebo: Making your Mind Matter* (New York: Hay House, 2014), 25-26.

[21] "Franz Anton Mesmer," http://www.anton-mesmer.com/.

In Mesmer's day, the power of faith ("self-suggestion") was key to the proposal, acceptance, and efficacy of his theory. However belief in Mesmer's theory lingered beyond his time, at one point being endorsed by *The New England Journal of Medicine*:

> Many positive reports of magnetism applied to nervous conditions and endorsements of autointoxication as the cause of mental diseases were, however, published in the *Journal*. Most of these quaint notions *simply reflected the medical ideologies* of the time.... [Mesmer's theory] "which some thirty years ago excited great attention... has since been viewed as one of the remarkable impositions on the credulity of mankind."[22]

Although the "medical ideology" of "animal magnetism" proposed by Mesmer and later taught by others would eventually be exposed as fraud, such a theory was believed to be valid and such belief even produced some efficacy.[23] It would take Louis XVI's committee, which included Benjamin Franklin, to ultimately expose Mesmer's biological theory as "nothing more than the power of imagination,"[24] what we now call the placebo effect.[25] However, for Mesmer and even for the modern medical community, faith and science have always been intermingled in forming constructs of mental illness and suggesting remedies. Still, modern psychiatrists and scientists have convinced many people that faith and science cannot legitimately coexist. Today, anyone who disagrees with or questions the current construct that holds to a physiological explanation of the soul is too often marginalized and labeled as uncaring. Jeffrey Oliver remarks,

---

[22] Allan H. Ropper, "Two Centuries of Neurology and Psychiatry in the Journal," *New England Journal of Medicine* 367 (July 5, 2012): 58-65.

[23] Lieberman, *Shrinks*, 29.

[24] Ibid.

[25] Dispenza, *You Are the Placebo*, 25-26.

> Indeed, to the modern psychiatric mind, rejecting the legitimacy of mental illness is not just an error but an act of inhumanity, leaving the sick without the hope of a cure. [They] are not just fools but monsters.[26]

However, there is a vast difference between rejecting the current construct of mental illness and denying that people have legitimate mental problems that need a remedy. One can reject the construct while still acknowledging and seeking to remedy mental struggles from a differing worldview.

Faith and science are not opposing realities and were once commonly understood and accepted to be harmonious and necessary elements of philosophy, anthropology, and sociology, that is, until Darwin introduced his theory of origins and the philosophy of materialism or positivism became widely accepted. The professor of psychiatry and atheist Thomas Szasz writes,

> In Europe in 1933, religion was not the enemy of science; scientism qua psychology and scientific materialism was. When people like Copernicus and Newton studied nature, they regarded their work in essentially religious terms. They were studying God's handiwork: created by God, the universe worked according to certain rules or laws; discovering what those laws were was a way to discover and know more about God. This outlook protected them from the scientistic political megalomania that came to dominate Freud's world, and ours.[27]

As we will discover and as Copernicus and Newton realized, acceptance of God's creation is paramount to having valid scientific views and conclusions. In fact (as Szasz observed), one's view of man's origin will determine his approach to science, to anthropology, and also to mental illness. Ultimately

---

[26] Jeffrey Oliver, "The Myth of Thomas Szasz," *New Atlantis*, no. 13 (Summer 2006): 68-84. Also available from http://www.thenewatlantis.com/publications/the-myth-of-thomas-szasz.

[27] Thomas Szasz, *Psychiatry: The Science of Lies* (New York: Syracuse University Press, 2008), 56.

such an unavoidable presuppositional faith establishes one's worldview and a subsequent construct of mental illness.

If in fact God created the world as He asserts, then He and His physical creation are not oppositional realties though their nature may differ. What God does oppose, however, is pseudo-science or scientism, which claims validity when none exists. What prominent figures within the mental health field often present as science amounts to a belief that the scientific process will one day provide empirical evidence to justify the current construct's continued acceptance. Sadly, this scientism or pseudoscience and faith in human wisdom undergird the current secular paradigm. In fact, Dr. Bessel van der Kolk remarks on his former Harvard University psychiatry professor's thinking:

> Our great teacher, Elvin Semrad, actively discouraged us from reading psychiatry textbooks during our first year. Semrad did not want our perceptions of reality to become obscured by the pseudocertainties of psychiatric diagnoses.[28]

As a whole, society has accepted these "pseudocertainties" and "pseudoscience" as if they were validated truth. But the current system of mental health not only lacks validity and is being questioned by a growing number of professionals;[29] it is also unproven and relatively new within history.

Though critical analysis of the current mental health paradigm are pressing and long overdue, its controversial nature has clouded the enormous need to discuss, define, and rely on a validated and proven paradigm of mental illness. This need becomes greater as the number of people identified with mental,

---

[28] Bessel van der Kolk, *The Body Keeps the Score: Brain, Mind, and Body in the Healing of Trauma* (New York: Penguin Group, 2014), 26.

[29] Richard Bentall, "Madness Explained: Why We Must Reject the Kraepelinian Paradigm and Replace It with a 'Complaint-Orientated' Approach to Understanding Mental Illness," *Medical Hypotheses* 66, no. 2 (2006): 220-33.

emotional, and behavioral problems grows each year. Christians are no exception, as churches are filled with people searching for help in regards to mental, emotional, and behavioral issues. The National Institute of Mental Health (NIMH) found in 2005 that

> an estimated 26.2 percent of Americans ages 18 and older — about one in four adults — suffer from a diagnosable mental disorder in a given year. When applied to the 2004 U.S. Census residential population estimate for ages 18 and older, this figure translates to 57.7 million people.[30]

Other research suggests that this problem is even more common than what the NIMH has reported,[31] and if statistical trends remain constant, another large increase should be expected. To make matters worse, people who are labeled as mentally ill, according to the director of the NIMH Thomas Insel, end up living on average twenty-three years less than those who are not identified as mentally ill.[32]

While we need to discuss mental illness and all issues surrounding the topic, we must also be precise in order to eliminate confusion. This clarity requires, at the outset, that we establish that *mental illness* is a broad construct which encompasses a wide variety of alleged disorders and diseases. Some of these proposed disorders are biological or neurological in nature and not actually mental (though such diseases can certainly influence thinking and affect behavior). Others are

---

[30] National Institute of Mental Health, "The Numbers Count: Mental Disorders in America," http://www.nimh.nih.gov/health/publications/the-numbers-count-mental-disorders-in-america/index.shtml. Other studies suggest 28%. See Jaak Panksepp, ed., *Textbook of Biological Psychiatry* (New York: John Wiley and Sons, 2004), 18.

[31] Charles L. Whitfield, *The Truth about Mental Illness: Choices for Healing* (Deerfield Beach, FL: Health Communications, 2004), preface xvi.

[32] Thomas Insel quoted by Liz Szabo, "A Manmade Disaster: A Mental Health System Drowning from Neglect," *USA Today* (May 12, 2014), http://www.usatoday.com/story/news/nation/2014/05/12/mental-health-system-crisis/7746535/.

theorized to be biologically-based and mental in nature (referred to as the brain-dysfunction theory), though no evidence for this hypothesis yet exists. Still others are clearly spiritual issues that are not biological at all (though such spiritual issues can certainly affect the physical brain and body). In other words, any practical and truly helpful definition of mental illness will take these critical distinctions into account. In fact, chief editor of the *Diagnostic and Statistical Manual-IV*, head of Duke University's school of psychiatry, and considered at the turn of the twenty-first century to be one of the most powerful psychiatrists in America, Allen Frances, remarks:

> I have reviewed dozens of definitions of mental disorder (and have written one myself in *DSM-IV*) and find none of them the slightest bit helpful either in determining which conditions should be considered mental disorders or not, or in deciding who is sick and who is not.[33]

He would later restate that "there is no definition of a mental disorder . . . I mean you can't define it."[34] Likewise, the former president-elect of the APA, Jeffery Lieberman recognizes that a definition of mental illness, especially one that fits everyone's opinion, is difficult to establish.[35] Dr. Karl Menninger also declares,

> To define illness and health is an almost impossible task. We can define mental illness as being a certain state of existence which is uncomfortable to someone. The suffering may be in the afflicted person or those around him or both, but a disturbance has occurred in the total economics of a personality.[36]

---

[33] Frances, *Saving Normal*, 17.

[34] Quoted by Gary Greenberg, *The Book of Woe: The DSM and the Unmaking of Psychiatry* (New York: Blue Rider Press, 2013), 23.

[35] Lieberman, *Shrinks*, 288-89.

[36] Karl Menninger, *The Vital Balance: The Life Process in Mental Health and Illness* (New York: Viking Press, 1968), 77.

Still others, such as Dr. Barbara Wootton, are more confident and believe that mental health should be defined as "ability to live happily, productively, without being a nuisance."[37]

Though we will sort through these differences, we need to be clear at the outset that mental illness is a social ideology or construct that is very broad and terms are not well-defined. Former trial clinicians for previous *DSMs*, Drs. Herb Kutchins and Stuart Kirk, explain:

> First, you must appreciate that the notion of mental disorder is what social scientists call a construct. Constructs are abstract concepts of something that is not real in the physical sense that a spoon or motorcycle or cat can be seen and touched. Constructs are shared ideas, supported by general agreement. . . . Mental illness is a construct. . . . The category itself is an invention, a creation. It may be a good and useful invention, or it may be a confusing one. *DSM* is a compendium of constructs. And like a large and popular mutual fund, *DSM*'s holdings are constantly changing as the *managers' estimates and beliefs about the value of those holdings change* [emphasis added]. . . . Some of these latest changes are rather difficult to decipher, as the constructs keep changing and multiplying like guppies. The constant revising provides the illusion that knowledge is changing rapidly.[38]

Like Kutchins and Kirk, the once-prominent and influential chair of the *DSM-IV* task force, Dr. Allen Francis, states, "We saw *DSM-IV* as a guidebook, not a bible—*a collection of temporarily useful diagnostic constructs, not a catalog of 'real' diseases* [emphasis added]."[39]

Although many believe that mental illness is a medical field, in truth, it is a construct that attempts to describe and approach common human mindsets, behaviors, and emotions through medicinal terms and means. A construct is simply a social theory

---

[37] Barbara Wootton, *Social Science and Social Pathology* (Putney, London: Allen & Unwin, 1968), 98.

[38] Herb Kutchins and Stuart A. Kirk, *Making Us Crazy: DSM: The Psychiatric Bible and the Creation of Mental Disorders* (New York: Free Press, 1997), 22-25.

[39] Frances, *Saving Normal*, 73.

built around or on an existing reality; it represents one way to describe and/or approach an issue or problem.

The current paradigm's ambiguity and imprecision have led to much confusion and hurt and facilitated its continued acceptance and place of authority. Furthermore, the reality that mental illness is a poorly defined construct has also led to avoidance within the church where there should be direct confrontation and empathetic help.

The church's lack of clear perspective, knowledge, and empathy represents an equally disappointing if not greater failure of God's people to offer help to believers and society as a whole. In many Bible-believing churches, care of the soul has been relinquished to secular professionals who claim to have biological coping-mechanisms readily available. As we will see, these failures are overwhelmingly the result of dismissing or ignoring the gospel and its practical application in people's lives. But the church can change the recent trend and become educated, empathetic, and responsible in providing God's answers to man's greatest needs.

While it is important that believers establish truth, it is also essential that they consider the genuine pain and suffering of others and approach them in love. In fact, without truth, we cannot love others as we should, and our care may cause further damage. Furthermore by discovering truth we are better equipped to offer genuine love. Truth and love represent the character of God and must guide all of our relationships and our thinking especially in regards to the discussion of the mind. Thus, in agreement with God's Word and wisdom, this series of books sets forth love and truth as essentials in dealing with such issues.

In order to accomplish our goals of both love and truth, we must base our construct of mental illness primarily on Scripture.

This necessity is not to say that we ignore science, for valid science further testifies of God's sovereign design according to His revealed Word.

Furthermore, we do not ignore the genuine pain and emotional hurt that has led to many being labeled as mentally ill. After all, the greatest commands are to love God and love others (Matthew 22:37-38).[40] Additionally, we cannot overlook (as the secular construct most often does) that a person's own character can cause him or her mental turmoil. As we understand God's truth about His design for humanity, we will learn how to love those with mental turmoil and anguish.

What complicates any endeavor by the church to become gospel-centered in its approach to mental illness is the existence of the well-established and heavily marketed secular paradigm. This popular secular view rests on overwhelming numbers of unanswered questions, ever-changing hypotheses, invalidated claims, outright deception, and, most troubling, the underlying worldview that denies both the existence of God and the spiritual/moral nature of humanity. The reality of the spiritual mind and its condition in the fallen world is a legitimate cause for careful consideration rather than blind acceptance.

To understand the true nature and premise of the secular construct of mental illness requires the discerning believer to examine history, alleged facts and theory, visible behaviors, objective neuroscience, and of course Scripture. From this exercise will emerge a valid understanding of human nature and an appropriate and reliable remedy for the human mind.

This series of books will begin that examination by answering foundational questions that are often overlooked or not logically considered, such as: Who decides what is normal

---

[40] The *ESV* is used throughout this book unless otherwise noted.

and abnormal? What is a definition of normalcy? Is the field of mental health a medical, scientific, or religious study? Who created the current construct of mental illness and why? Are humans strictly material, spiritual, or are they psychosomatic in nature? What is the mind-brain connection?

Once these important questions are answered, the series will explore the underlying philosophy that governs the current paradigm of mental illness and focus on providing an understanding of the brain-dysfunction theory as well as how the issue of nurture must be considered. We will also compare secularist's ideas with God's wisdom about the same mindsets, emotions, and behaviors. To end our discussion, we will examine not only what remedies are suggested by secularists and Scripture, but also explore what causes efficacy/healing in each suggested treatment.

What I intend to argue is that faith, authority, and dependence are relevant and even vital issues in our discussion of mental illness. Furthermore, my prayer is that this series of books will help those who minister to others in need to be better equipped to provide hope and lasting change that benefits the counselee, helps better society, and glorifies God.

Finally, I encourage Christians to be gracious in their dialogue and interactions with others who do not hold to similar positions, especially those who have embraced the current construct. Christians can certainly choose to disagree, but they cannot forsake the reality that they are not fighting other people, but, as will be discussed, Christians are wrestling against spiritual darkness and worldly powers.

While we may walk away from conversations in disagreement, we must all be resolute to graciously interact and communicate God's love and truth to those around us. The gospel of Jesus Christ demands that we exalt God's truth, love each other, and expose and reject all doctrines and philosophies which oppose the gospel of Jesus Christ; these are the goals of this project.

INTRODUCTION

"Your beliefs define your vision of the world; they dictate your behavior; they determine your emotional responses to other human beings.... They become part of the very apparatus of your mind, determining your desires, fears, expectations and subsequent behavior."[41] – neuroscientist and atheist, Sam Harris

"It is not gene-directed hormones and neurotransmitters that control our bodies and our minds; our beliefs control our bodies, and our minds, and thus our lives."[42] – former research professor at Stanford University Medical Center, Bruce Lipton

Imagine seeing a close friend who had been a happy and outgoing person; however, when you meet him this time, he fails to recognize you or any of his other friends. In fact he seems to struggle to remember his own identity. As you begin to talk with him, you realize that he has become uncharacteristically irritable, irresponsible, and withdrawn. He acts anxious and dissociated around you, and when he does talk, his speech is slurred. Furthermore, within brief conversations, his mood swings are surprisingly extreme: he exhibits deep sorrow and weeping and then suddenly becomes irate and aggressive. His whole person seems to be enveloped by deep anxiety, and his words and behavior indicate that he is delirious.

---

[41] Sam Harris, *The End of Faith: Religion, Terror, and the Future of Reason* (New York: Norton and Company, 2005), 12.

[42] Bruce H. Lipton, *The Biology of Belief: Unleashing the Power of Consciousness, Matter & Miracles* (New York: Hay House, 2005), preface xxvi.

Observations may indicate that this individual is mentally ill and that he needs medication and professional therapy, especially if these behavioral patterns persist. Some may even conclude that he is demon-possessed. These conclusions stem from preconceived ideas about human behavior that are now prevalent and accepted to be true. If, however, we investigate this man's history and the true cause of such behaviors, an entirely different diagnosis/ judgment may very well emerge.

In actuality, the man previously described is not mentally ill or demon-possessed as we might expect; he is instead sleep-deprived. In fact, the description supplied above contains common symptoms in most sleep-deprived soldiers, and these specific symptoms are taken directly from the book *On Killing* written by West Point professor and retired soldier Dave Grossman.[43] Had we known this man's life context and more information about who he was prior to our evaluation, we could have made a more accurate judgment and realized a more profitable remedy to his seemingly irrational existence. Yet, our perceptions founded upon our beliefs — whether in the current secular construct of mental illness or not — guided our thinking toward interpreting this man's condition.

The current construct of mental illness demands that we believe a person's testimony or judge their behavior often without considering their moral character or fully understanding their history. While our evaluation is based on our interpretation of other's behavior, our interpretation is based on our faith in a social/religious construct. The science of mental illnesses is limited to observing only physical characteristics, behavior, and biological effects in order to form judgments. This reality makes

---

[43] Dave Grossman, *On Killing: the Psychological Cost of Learning to Kill in War and Society*, rev. ed. (New York: Back Bay Books, 2009), 45.

faith essential to understanding immaterial realities of man—such as the mind—that cannot be physically observed. As we will also see, the limitation of science to the physical nature of man also tends toward confusing causes and effects both in observing the individual and forming a valid-standardized anthropology.

Because observations apart from God's wisdom are all that science possesses to evaluate and theorize about humanity, secularists often claim science to be the only viable approach to defining and describing humanity. In fact, the current accepted secular system of judgment or diagnosis prefers to fit people into categories according to their behavior rather than to explore the individual's character, their biographical uniqueness, and the true causes of their problems.[44] But in fairness, no one is able to observe and discern the human mind/spiritual heart; only God can: "The heart is deceitful above all things and desperately sick [lit. 'incurably sick']; who can understand it? I the LORD search the heart and test the mind, to give every man according to his ways, according to the fruit of his deeds" (Jeremiah 17:9).[45] It is impossible for people to search out the spiritual heart or mind, and this fact makes trusting God's discernment and understanding all the more important. But accepting or rejecting God's discernment of the mind/spiritual heart also requires faith.

---

[44] "The first [characteristic of the current system] relates to the refusal of many mental health professionals (including some psychiatrists) to concede naturalism and its purported categories of mental illness and to favor instead dynamic wholism, biographical uniqueness, and continua rather than categories" (Vikram Patel, et. al., *Mental and Neurological Public Health: A Global Perspective* [San Diego: Academic Press, 2010], 477).

[45] See Appendix B for examples on how we are commonly deceived.

Observable behaviors and neurological activity in the brain do not explain the mind nor do they offer a complete anthropology. Yet these observable human realities are the fundamental empirical evidence upon which the secular construct of mental illness rests. But behavior and neurological activity can just as easily be explained by other means. The current accepted paradigm of mental illness more offers a secular philosophy of anthropology and a subsequent system of behavioral categorization within evolution than it does provide objective answers and valid remedies to the human mind.

After all, secularists admit that they continue to search for valid causes, efficient remedies, and validating proof concerning their larger theory of mental illness and all of their individual psychiatric labels.[46] While these necessary answers are lacking, secularists must still explain and fit people's unwanted or impairing behaviors, mindsets, desires, and emotions into their evolutionary thinking. Thus their construct of mental illness becomes a necessity, attempting to explain moral and social aspects of anthropology that do not otherwise fit into their evolutionary worldview. Renowned secular psychiatrist Peter Breggin remarks, "When we don't understand and accept the context of a human experience, and especially when it seems harmful or bad and lasts a long time, we tend to label it mental illness."[47] Similarly, professor of psychiatry and atheist Thomas Szasz states that the idea of mental illness is a metaphor used by secularists to describe man's internal difficulties in dealing with

---

[46] Frances, *Saving Normal*, 10.

[47] Peter R. Breggin, *Toxic Psychiatry* (New York: St. Martin's Press, 1991), 136.

"moral conflicts."[48] Like Breggin and Szasz, professor of sociology, Thomas Scheff, also sees the modern construct of mental illness as a way to describe what humanists (through the lens of evolutionary thinking) cannot explain or understand about the complexities of people.[49] In many ways, the secular paradigm of mental illness is a Darwinian catch-all to explain distressed or impaired aspects of the human immaterial nature.

It is no surprise, then, that these subjective judgments of common human behavior continue to expand into every aspect of human life. If any behavior, mindset, or emotion impairs a person's life, it is most likely considered to be a disease within the current construct. Jeffery Oliver explains,

> The only way to diagnose this "disease," or any other mental illness, remains the observation of behavior. Given the complexity of the human psyche, this makes sense: we can hardly expect the many moods and miseries of human life, even the most extreme, to have simple neurological explanations. But given the grand ambitions of modern psychiatry — to explain the human condition, to heal every broken soul — the reliance on behavioral observation has led to the medicalization of an ever-growing range of human behaviors. It treats life's difficulties and oddities as clinical conditions rather than humanity in its fullness.[50]

But there is more to consider than behavior, and the discerning individual will seek the root cause of seemingly unusual behavior.

Any approach to man's mind, including the current secular construct of mental illness, requires faith. Former president-elect

---

[48] Thomas Szasz, "The Myth of Mental Illness," *American Psychologist* 15 (1960): 113-18. See also Thomas Szasz, *The Myth of Psychotherapy: Mental Healing as a Religion, Rhetoric, and Repression* (New York: Anchor Press, 1978).

[49] Thomas J. Scheff, *Being Mentally Ill: A Sociological Theory* (Chicago: Aldine, 1966).

[50] Jeffery Oliver, "The Myth of Thomas Szasz," *New Atlantis* no. 13 (Summer 2006): 68-84, http://www.thenewatlantis.com/publications/the-myth-of-thomas-szasz.

of the American Psychiatric Association (APA), Jeffrey Lieberman, remarks,

> Psychiatry's attempts to help the public distinguish evidence-based treatments from unsubstantiated fabrications have long been inadequate, and remain so today. You may wonder how thousands of educated intelligent people—teachers, scientists, and business people, as well as court reporters—*could have ever believed* that an invisible network of orgasmic energy was the key to mental health. Yet even now, *charlatans drawn from the ranks of professional psychiatry continue to dupe desperate and unsuspecting patients* as the institutions of psychiatry passively stand by [emphasis added].[51]

Although Lieberman criticizes belief in false theories, faith is required to accept any psychiatric theory about the mind.

The Necessity of Faith

To construct any theory of mental illness requires a presupposition of and an ongoing reliance on faith rather than science. This reality is what Dr. Thomas Szasz notes when he describes the history of psychiatry during the nineteenth century: "Roughly between 1850-1880, malingering became transformed into hysteria, and psychiatry—increasingly distinct from neurology—became a popular belief system, a medical-secular religion."[52] Though touted as issues of science and medicine, finding and applying a remedy to people's mental problems are faith-based endeavors.

Science is certainly relevant, but every person's interpretation and beliefs about physical observations stem from his or her worldview. Former Stanford University researcher Bruce Lipton asserts,

> Learning how to harness your mind to promote growth is the secret of life.... Of course the secret of life is not a secret at all. Teachers like Buddha and Jesus have been telling us the same story for

---

[51] Lieberman, *Shrinks*, 21.

[52] Szasz, *Psychiatry*, 18.

> millennia. Now science is pointing in the same direction. It is not our genes but our beliefs that control our lives.... Oh ye of little belief![53]

Faith, then, is the keynote discussion, not a side issue, when it comes to the mind. Of course, the idea that faith is the premiere topic in the field of mental health contradicts and undermines the core of the brain-dysfunction theory. Still, many secular professionals understand that their field is not strictly scientific. Psychiatrist Peter Breggin explains,

> Psychiatry is neither pure science nor medicine. It's a mishmash of philosophy, psychology, religion, law enforcement, politics as well as social engineering and big business, and occasionally science and medicine.[54]

The chair of the *DSM-IV* task force, Allen Frances also remarks,

> Psychiatric diagnosis is seeing something that exists, but with a pattern shaped by what we expect to see [presuppositional faith]. Because there is no one right way, fashions prevail. The ancient shaman had different names and explanations — but these worked almost as well for him as current names and explanations work for the modern shrink.[55]

Similarly, Ethan Watters states,

> The diversity [in ideas of mental illness] that can be found across cultures can be seen across time as well. Because the troubled mind has been perceived in terms of diverse religious, scientific, and social beliefs of discrete cultures, the forms of madness from one place and time in history often look remarkably different from the forms of madness in another.[56]

For the Christian counselor or the secular psychiatrist, it is faith that determines positions and practices.

---

[53] Lipton, *Biology of Belief,* preface xxvi.

[54] Breggin, *Toxic Psychiatry*, 381-82.

[55] Frances, *Saving Normal*, 36.

[56] Ethan Watters, *Crazy Like Us: The Globalization of the American Psyche* (New York: Free Press, 2010), 2.

Faith is not only the basis of psychiatry, it is also the grounds for acceptance of the brain-dysfunction theory. Neuroscientist and atheist Sam Harris strongly advocates the brain-dysfunction theory; however, he believes that faith is detrimental to humanity's well-being. In the opening of his book *The End of Faith*, Harris attempts to establish the danger and destructive nature of human faith:

> Your beliefs define your vision of the world; they dictate your behavior; they determine your emotional responses to other human beings. . . . They become part of the very apparatus of your mind, determining your desires, fears, expectations and subsequent behavior.[57]

Harris' attempt to attack faith undermines his own belief in the brain-dysfunction theory by revealing that faith causes emotions, desires, fears, expectations, and behavior. Modern psychiatrists' view that the brain or genetics is responsible for behavioral, emotional, and mental struggles makes the conversation appear to be scientific and medical. But such a claim requires significant faith in unproven theories and an evolutionary worldview. Psychiatrist Sally Satel and psychologist Scott Lilienfeld attest, "The brain-disease model [foundational to the current construct] has become dogma—and like *all articles of faith*, it is typically *believed* without question [emphasis added]."[58]

Contemporary physicians are not alone in understanding that theories of mental health are not strictly scientific endeavors. Both Sigmund Freud and Carl Jung realized that faith is essential to any discussion about the immaterial nature:

---

[57] Harris, *End of Faith*, 12.

[58] Sally Satel and Scott Lilienfeld, *Brainwashed: The Seductive Appeal of Mindless Neuroscience* (New York: Basic Books, 2013), 50.

> The controversy over whether psychotherapy belongs to medicine or religion is not new. Freud and Jung devoted a great deal of attention to this problem, claiming psychotherapy sometimes for medicine, sometimes for religion.[59]

It may also surprise the reader to learn how frequently secularists describe their practices as an almost-religious endeavor. For example, Mark Micale and Roy Porter note of psychiatry that it is "a new psychosomatic-religious-ethical-scientific medicine."[60] Others, such as psychiatrist William Sargant in his celebrated book *Battle for the Mind*, insist that "politicians, priests and psychiatrists often face the same problem: how to find the most rapid and permanent means of changing a man's beliefs."[61] To Sargant, treatment of psychological problems was a matter of "conversion" but by physiological and mechanical means. He himself had been persuaded by his own mental anguish that the brain was the cause of mental struggles, and he was ready to "proselytize the outside world."[62] Similarly the 1960s textbook *Abnormal Psychology: Mental Illness Types, Causes, and Treatment* says,

> The problem of mental disorder is probably as old as man. Recorded history reports a broad range of interpretations of abnormal behavior and methods for its alleviation or eradication, which have generally reflected the degree of enlightenment and the trends of *religious, philosophical,* and *social beliefs* and practices of the times [emphasis added].[63]

---

[59] Thomas Szasz, *The Myth of Psychotherapy: Mental Healing as a Religion, Rhetoric, and Repression* (New York: Anchor Press, 1978), 179.

[60] Mark Micale and Roy Porter, eds., *Discovering the History of Psychiatry* (New York: Oxford University Press, 1994), 43.

[61] William Sargant, *Battle for the Mind: A Physiology of Conversion and Brainwashing* (New York: Harper and Row, 1971), 37.

[62] Ibid., 37, 48-49.

[63] Coville, Costello, and Rouke, *Abnormal Psychology*, 11.

Truly, faith is not merely a side topic in the discussion of mental illness: it is the foundational issue.

But we must not merely discuss how faith is necessary to hold to any construct of mental illness, we also must logically and practically work through foundational issues relating to faith. Such an endeavor may very well begin in one's definition of mental illness.

In contrast to renowned secular psychiatrists, such as Allen Frances, who sees defining mental illness as well-nigh impossible,[64] *Merriam-Webster's Dictionary* defines mental illness as "a mental or bodily condition marked primarily by *sufficient disorganization* of personality, mind, and emotions to seriously impair the *normal psychological functioning of the individual* [emphasis added]."[65] Likewise, the fifth edition of the *Diagnostic and Statistical Manual of Mental Disorders* (hereafter referred to as DMS-5) defines mental illness as:

> a syndrome characterized by *clinically significant disturbance* in an individual's cognition, emotion regulation, or behavior that reflects a dysfunction in the psychological, biological, or developmental processes underlying mental function. Mental disorders are usually associated with *significant distress* or disability in social, occupational, or other important activities . . . [emphasis added][66]

Such widely accepted definitions of mental illness, however, raise logical questions that require valid answers: (1) what constitutes "normal psychological functioning of the individual" or "clinically significant disturbances"? and (2) who has the authority to decide what is sufficient organization and normal

---

[64] Greenberg, *Book of Woe*, 23.

[65] www.merriam-webster.com/medical/mental%20disorder.

[66] American Psychiatric Association, *The Diagnostic and Statistical Manual of Mental Disorders*, 5th ed. (Washington, DC: American Psychiatric Publishing, 2013), 20.

psychological functioning? In addition to these questions, two related questions could also be proposed: who decides what is sufficient disorganization, and who defines clinically significant disturbances? These questions are important and legitimate, and many prominent psychiatrists are beginning to ask them:

> Who gets to define what is "complete" physical, mental, and social well-being? Is someone sick because his body aches from hard work or he feels sad after a disappointment or is in a family feud? And are the poor inherently sicker because they have fewer resources to achieve the complete well-being required of "health"?[67]

Each of these questions leads the discussion further toward the undeniable reality of faith and the necessity to establish some authority. But it is impossible for science alone to answer these foundational questions, since the scientific process is limited to observing and testing mankind's physical nature.[68]

Still, secularists who believe the construct of mental illness are certain that "inquiry into the brain will eventually and exhaustively explain the mind and, hence, human nature. Ultimately ... neuroscience will—and should—dictate human values."[69] Can fields of science truly dictate man's values, morality, and see into the inward facets of mankind as God does? Can science or medicine fully define normalcy? Any answers to these important questions will require faith.

The Necessity of Authority

Discussions on mental illness must begin not only with establishing faith but also with establishing an authority on human behavior, mindsets, and emotions. In other words, who

---

[67] Frances, *Saving Normal*, 9.

[68] David Eagleman, *The Brain: The Story of You* (New York: Pantheon Books, 2015), 32.

[69] Satel and Lilienfeld, *Brainwashed*, introduction xviii.

has the right/privilege of determining what the standard of normalcy is for being human? Determining authority and a standard of normalcy will ultimately be based on a person's view of origins.

People can choose to place their faith either in the secular worldview and the current authorities or in the biblical worldview and the authority of God. Undergirding the current construct of mental illness is the belief that humans are a product of evolution, environment, and genetics and that people are inherently good, entirely physical in nature, and therefore not responsible for their behavior.[70] In contrast, the biblical explanation of man presents humanity as a direct creation of God, entirely depraved, culpable for wrongdoing, and living in a world that is passing away.[71] Since these two presuppositional

---

[70] Kendra Cherry, "What is Humanistic Psychology?" http://psychology.about.com/od/historyofpsychology/a/hist_humanistic.htm.

[71] We must dispel the widely held but incorrect theory, which proposes that mental illness was God's or the gods' judgments on man. (Andrew Scull, *Madness in Civilization: A Cultural History of Insanity from the Bible to Freud, from the Madhouse to Modern Medicine* [Princeton: Princeton University Press 2015]). The biblical worldview is far different from this wrong way of thinking. While there are cases of mental anguish in Scripture that are a result of God's judgment on man's pride (such as observed in the case of King Nebuchadnezzar), these recorded events are portrayed as unusual situations. Yet, many historians and secularists focus on such atypical historical events in characterizing the biblical position, conveniently ignoring that they reflect only a very small portion of the Bible's thorough and nuanced anthropology and explanations of mental anguish and turmoil. The *American Psychiatric Publishing Textbook of Forensic Psychiatry* attests to such a predominant representation of religious approaches: "The asylums of the nineteenth century were a new phenomenon. . . . Naturalistic and secular explanations of human behavior replaced mystical or divine explanations. . . . Explanations of insanity, which had previously been considered a demonstration of divine intervention or punishment, also began to reflect a rational, humanistic perspective. By the mid-eighteenth century, madness came to be considered a pathological condition that could be cured" (Robert Simon and Liza Gold, eds., *The American Psychiatric Publishing Textbook of Forensic Psychiatry* [Washington, DC: American Psychiatric Publishing, 2010], 11). As we will see, this common secular view of God and His Word is a gross misrepresentation of the biblical perspective.

views of anthropology are antithetical, the integration of these two approaches is impossible. Yet, one of these worldviews undergirds every approach to the mind and mental struggles.

CHAPTER 1 – DECIDING NORMALCY IN MENTAL ILLNESS

One of the most important matters in any theory or construct of mental illness is a clearly defined standard of normalcy. Although establishing a definition of normalcy is of the upmost importance in order to suggest a deviance or abnormality, the topic is too often ignored or marginalized in discussions. Yet proposed disorders, diagnoses, etiologies, and remedies all depend upon this key anthropological starting point. Even claims of scientific validity and reliability depend first upon establishing a standard of what it means to be human before suggesting and testing theories of disorder.

The secular construct of mental illness—owned by the American Psychiatric Association (APA) and expressed in the *DSM-5*—represents the most widely accepted attempt to understand and define humanity within the philosophical framework of evolutionary ideology. The former president-elect of the APA, Jeffery Lieberman explains,

> Psychiatry has become deeply ingrained within the fabric of our culture, winding through our most prominent social institutions and coloring our most mundane daily encounters. For better or worse, the *DSM* is not merely a compendium of medical diagnoses. *It has become a public document that helps define how we understand ourselves and how we live our lives* [emphasis added].[72]

Likewise, clinical psychologist Richard Bentall explains the close connection between studying perceived mental illness and the nature of humanity itself:

> I have found myself exploring surprising avenues, such as, for example, developmental psychology, medical anthropology, the new

---

[72] Lieberman, *Shrinks*, 291.

> molecular genetics, developmental neurobiology and ideas from the branch of mathematics known as non-linear dynamics. These explorations have confirmed . . . that psychosis shines a particularly penetrating light on ordinary human functioning. *Indeed, I do not think it is an exaggeration to say that the study of psychosis amounts to the study of human nature* [emphasis added].[73]

What is considered normal human nature and variances from this standard are inseparable discussions in regards to a construct of mental illness.

As foundational as the issue of normalcy is, it may be surprising that the authorities over the current construct of mental illness offer no clear definition or standard of normalcy. In fact, as Lieberman and Bentall attest, the *DSM* represents a great portion of psychiatry's proposed anthropology, yet it ignores vital discussion on normalcy and instead focuses on defining and categorizing alleged abnormalities. *DSM-III* task force member Z.J. Liposwski explains "the proper scope of psychiatry":

> Its core focus is on abnormal experience and behavior of persons that cause suffering for them or for others, or both. As physicians, our role is to diagnose and treat such abnormalities. Yet what is considered abnormal changes over time and hence the boundaries of our field are fluid.[74]

Professor of psychiatry, Thomas Szasz also remarks,

> The basic science of human actions are, therefore, anthropology and sociology, for it is these disciplines that are concerned with exhibiting, in a systematic manner, the framework of norms and goals which are necessary to classify actions as being of a certain sort. Psychiatry and psychoanalysis, too, deal with these problems, although they often do so inexplicitly [75]

---

[73] Bentall, *Madness Explained*, 111.

[74] Z.J. Lipowski, "Psychiatry: Mindless or Brainless, Both or Neither?" *Canadian Journal of Psychiatry* 34 (3) (1989): 249-54.

[75] Szasz, *Myth of Psychotherapy*, 149.

Psychiatrists and psychologists form theories of human behavior that amount to inexplicit theories of anthropology and sociology. Instead of clearly defining and stating what it means to be human, they choose instead to assert what it means to be abnormal.

But even the APA's suggestions on what it means to be abnormal as expressed in the *DSM-5* are imprecise. The APA admits that:

> In the absence of clear biological markers or clinically useful measurements of severity for many mental disorders, it has not been possible to completely separate normal and pathological symptom [abnormal] expressions contained in the diagnostic criteria.[76]

When it comes to the unobservable human mind, normal and abnormal states are not easily delineated or defined, and within the current ideology, they are often ambiguous.

A Secular Definition of Normal

Abnormality cannot truly be determined until a standard of normalcy is established and upheld. The current authorities overseeing the construct of mental illness assume that a line of demarcation exists between normal and abnormal behavior, though they have yet to provide it apart from the subjective approach of utilitarianism.[77] One of the leading authorities on the psychiatric construct of Attention Deficit Hyperactivity Disorder (ADHD), Russell Barkley, affirms in his book that an established anthropology precludes any theory of mental illness or abnormal pathology:

> Any theory of child psychopathological condition such as ADHD will ultimately have to be linked to larger theories of the nature of normal developmental psychological processes and the neuropsychological processes that comprise them. *Pathological states*

---

[76] APA, *DSM-5*, 21.

[77] Frances, *Saving Normal*, 5.

> *are variations from normal states.* An understanding of the development of those normal psychological functions, therefore, can provide substantial insight into the development of the psychopathological condition. In short, the literature about psychological disorder and that about its normal developmental counterpart must be bridged at some point in theory construction. . . . Consequently, any theory of ADHD is, of necessity, a theory of executive functions and self-regulation [emphasis added].[78]

Similarly, Dr. Ed Tronick, a professor of developmental and brain sciences at the University of Massachusetts Boston comments on the absurdity of labeling very young children as disordered: "There's this very narrow range of what people think the prototype child should look like [normal]. Deviations from that lead them to seek out interventions like these [psychiatric remedies]."[79] However the current mental health system has only an ambiguous notion of the normal child as well as the normal adult. Dr. Bentall also touches on the inexistent demarcation of what it means to be normal vs. abnormal within the secular construct of mental illness:

> The differences between those who are diagnosed as suffering from a psychiatric disorder and those who are not amounts to not very much. This is an important insight because of its implications for psychiatric care.[80]

If the necessary standard of normalcy is not well-defined or established, how then can deviations or abnormalities be proposed? Secular psychiatrist Lawrie Reznek understands this to be one of the most critical questions of psychiatry:

---

[78] Russell A. Barkley, *ADHD and the Nature of Self-Control* (New York: Guilford, 2005), vii-viii.

[79] Allen Schwarz, "Still in a Crib, Yet Being Given Antipsychotics," *New York Times* (December 10, 2015), http://mobile.nytimes.com/2015/12/11/us/psychiatric-drugs-are-being-prescribed-to-infants.html?referer=&_r=1.

[80] Bentall, *Madness Explained,* 123.

> If parents can judge their son as mentally ill when he doesn't want to do what they consider normal, then the question arises as to how much of what we call mental illness is driven by social norms imposed on perfectly normal and healthy individuals. If you like, this is the fundamental question of psychiatry. It is of critical importance, not only because we don't want to waste valuable resources on trying to treat normal people squashed into flawed disease categories, and divert those resources from more needy patients, but also because psychiatric treatments are not without their hazards, as the history of psychiatry abundantly demonstrates.[81]

An accepted definition and idea of human normalcy must first be understood and clearly defined before abnormalities can be determined, categorized, and diagnosed. This need applies not only to the mental health construct, but to all aspects of man. Reznek stresses this point in regards to man's morality and character: "We need an understanding of evil character before we can understand excuses in general and insanity in particular."[82] Normalcy, then (no matter how it is defined), is the consistent standard and abnormalities are the deviations; therefore, a precise definition of normalcy must precede any description or suggestion of abnormality.

However any definition of normalcy has as its basis an established worldview. Everyone must choose to embrace either the changing and often-conflicting human theories/constructs or the unchanging wisdom of the Creator. The choice for either the human or divine perspective requires faith and establishes an authority in matters of anthropology.

Unfortunately, the secular presupposition of mental illness permeates our society and indirectly shapes many believers' thinking. But to accept the secular construct of mental illness demands that the presuppositional and unbiblical anthropology

---

[81] Reznek, *Peddling Mental Disorder*, 1.

[82] Lawrie Reznek, *Evil or Ill?: Justifying the Insanity Defense* (New York: Routledge, 1997), 14.

on which the construct is built also be accepted. For example, evolutionary theory views man as amoral, not responsible for mental struggles, reactions to bad experiences, character flaws, or poor relationships. Within evolutionary thinking, people are perceived as strong and good. When an individual's mindsets, emotions, or behavior appear to cause mental strain, distress or impairment, then that person is viewed as abnormal and theorized to be ill. These impairments or states of distress—as presented in the *DSM* and according to the current construct—are argued to be abnormal human characteristics which cannot be controlled. Robert Whitaker explains,

> There is one other, subtler aspect to his epidemic. Over the past twenty-five years, psychiatry has profoundly reshaped our society. Through its *Diagnostic and Statistical Manual*, psychiatry draws a line between what is "normal" and what is not. Our societal understanding of the human mind, which in the past arose from a medley of sources (great works of fiction, scientific investigations, and philosophical and religious writings), is now filtered through the *DSM*. Indeed, the stories told by psychiatry about "chemical imbalances" in the brain have reshaped our understanding of how the mind works and challenged our conceptions of free will. Are we really the prisoners of our neurotransmitters?[83]

In spite of the *DSM's* wide acceptance, it represents not a standard of normalcy but a humanistic classification of perceived abnormalities and theorized biological defects.

While the *DSM* may imply an evolutionary standard of normal, many psychologists and licensed therapists are seeking to form their own definitions of normal and establish their own authoritative classification systems.[84] One of the largest groups

---

[83] Robert Whitaker, *Anatomy of an Epidemic: Magic Bullets, Psychiatric Drugs, and the Astonishing Rise of Mental Illness in America* (New York: Broadway Books, 2015), 10.

[84] The *ICD* is owned by the World Health Organization and could someday replace the *DSM* as the world-wide authority. There is a large movement—especially within psychology—to make the *ICD* the standard of mental illness diagnosis. American Psychology Association, "ICD vs. DSM," *Monitor on Psychology* 40, no. 9 (Oct 2009): 63.

making inroads into the APA's monopoly over the mental health system and offering a concise definition of normalcy is the World Health Organization (WHO). The WHO asserts its own terms and approaches to psychiatric disorders, but its existence and potential place of authority are based entirely on the *DSM*.[85] Unlike the APA and their *DSM*, however, WHO defines mental health—and thus normalcy—with specificity: "mental health is a state of complete physical, mental, and social well-being and not merely the absence of infirmity."[86] Dr. Allen Francis recognizes that such an anthropological view places everyone into the category of being abnormal and mentally ill since all are fallible. Francis rejects the WHO's definition of normalcy and instead suggests that utilitarianism—which allegedly seeks the "greatest good for the greatest number"[87]—is the only valid way to approach humanity and establish a definition or standard of normalcy. He explains,

> Utilitarianism provided the first, and remains the only practical philosophic guidance on how and where to set a boundary between "normal" and "mental disorder." The guiding assumptions are that "normal" has no universal meaning and can never be defined with precision by the spinning wheels of philosophical deduction—it is very much in the eye of the beholder and is changeable over time, place, and cultures. From this it follows that the boundary separating "normal" from "mental disorder" should be based not on abstract reasoning, but rather on the balance between the positive and the negative consequences that accrue from different choices.[88]

Such a wrong philosophy and convenient mantra permits practitioners to subjectively change their minds while claiming altruism as their motive for everything they do, even if such

---

[85] American Psychology Association, "ICD vs. DSM," 63.

[86] World Health Organization, http://www.who.int/trade/glossary/story046/en/.

[87] Frances, *Saving Normal*, 5.

[88] Ibid.

practices are harmful and lack understanding of long-term-effects.[89] Psychiatrists assert that they practice science and medicine, but in truth, they place their faith in the philosophy of utilitarianism, materialism, and determinism, all of which stem from their evolutionary worldview.

Furthermore, psychiatric utilitarianism amounts to evolutionary pragmatism—relying on the majority's (or at least the current authority's) accepted opinion. In fact, many professionals disagree with the opinion of the current APA leadership. Psychiatrists Til Wykes and Felicity Callard comment on this reality: "Most of these changes [to the *DSM-5*] imply a more inclusive system of diagnoses where the pool of 'normality' shrinks to a mere puddle."[90] If normalcy is a subjective opinion as prominent secular authorities claim, then whoever is given the greatest authority has the privilege of deciding normalcy. What Drs. Wykes and Callard's comments also recognize is that normal people could easily be labeled abnormal within the secular construct.

The reality that the authorities residing over the secular construct choose not to state a clear definition of normalcy and

---

[89] While the intentions of individual secularists may very well be the good of those they meet, the paradigm is not focused on the needs of the individual, but on maintaining the current construct and dealing with everyday social issues. Rosemond and Ravenel note this reality in discussing ADHD: "In short, the disease model serves the interests of the parents, the therapist, the prescribing physician, and the manufacturer(s) of the drug(s) prescribed. The only person the disease model does not benefit is the child" (John Rosemond and Bose Ravenel, *The Diseasing of America's Children: Exposing the ADHD Fiasco and Empowering Parents to Take Back Control* [Nashville: Thomas Nelson, 2008], 75). Most convincing, however, is that according to their own admission, no remedy yet exists for any of their proposed disorders. This fact translates into a 0% success rate of healing. In spite of this mind-boggling failure, many still place their faith and confidence in the neo-Kraepelinian construct.

[90] Til Wykes and Felicity Callard, "Diagnosis, Diagnosis, Diagnosis: Towards DSM-5," *Journal of Mental Health* 19, no. 4 (2010).

instead practice the ever-changing belief system of utilitarianism is precisely what Dr. Reznek points out has led to a "hazardous history," which continues to produce the same failing and dangerous results.[91] Still, psychiatrists wish to view and market themselves as "*psychopharmacologists*, empathic prescribers of medication."[92] The truth, however, is that the secular definition of normal on which the *DSM* and secular construct of mental illness exists is an ambiguous ideology governed by utilitarianism and the evolutionary theory. In other words, the current construct of mental illness is a dangerous fallacy which enables the creation of alleged illnesses from perceived deviances — even though the vital standard of measurement is ambiguous and undisclosed.

The Biblical Definition of Normal

In contrast to the absence or inexactness of the *DSM's* definition of normalcy, the biblical position is precise. It is based on theology and the creation account. In fact, one of the main tenets of the Bible is to reveal not only a right theology but also a corresponding anthropology; God intends these two studies to be interrelated. Whether or not the Bible's claims of normalcy are accepted, one must at least concede that it establishes a clear description of what constitutes "normal psychological functioning of the individual."[93] In order to discover what is normal — and subsequently what is mental illness, we must consider what the Scripture teaches about God and man.

---

[91] Reznek, *Peddling Mental Disorder*, 1.

[92] Lieberman, *Shrinks*, 193.

[93] http://www.merriam-webster.com/medical/mental%20disorder.

Scripture sets forth two perspectives of normalcy. The first perspective is God's original intent for all of mankind that we be perfect and in right relationships with God and man. The second definition or perspective is our common or normal human nature and shared condition of our minds. Though they are two different ways of looking at one reality, these perspectives both lead to the same conclusion about mankind's true nature and define what it means to be a normal human being.

The first perspective is God the Father's original intent for mankind, which establishes normal as the perfect person of Jesus Christ and how God intended man to live. Christ was fully God and fully human but without sin. Since God is the ultimate authority, then His will and desire matter most. With God's original intent for man in mind, you could also say that normal looks like Adam prior to the fall and before the effects of sin. This understanding is theologically sound, since our suffering and mental and relational problems are sourced in the corporate fall through Adam (Romans). God's standard of normalcy is perfection. When mankind became imperfect—because of sin entering the world—everyone's mental state was in immediate need of restoration and spiritual healing (Romans 1; 12:1-2). So God's perspective of the human mind is that each person's fallen condition requires that they be restored to the image of Christ or to the pre-fall Adam (1 Corinthians 15:22, 45-49; Hebrews 9:14).

In accordance with this biblical understanding, the World Health Organization's (WHO) definition of mental health not only makes sense, it also determines each individual to be abnormal when compared to Christ who was perfect in every way. We recall that the WHO defines mental health as "a state of complete, physical, mental, and social well-being."[94] Since the

---

[94] Frances, *Saving Normal*, 9.

fall of Adam during the creation account, everyone experiences both their own depraved nature and the consequences of the fallen world around them. In the metaphorical sense—which the Bible establishes as the second perspective, then, everyone is mentally ill. Most secularists reject the WHO's definition of mental health, because they reject the notion that anyone fits the description of perfection. Dr. Allen Frances explains,

> Who among us would dare claim health if it requires meeting this impossibly high standard [of the WHO]? Health loses value as a concept when it is so unobtainable that everyone is at least partly sick. The definition also excludes culture and context-sensitive value judgments . . . . More realistic modern definitions of health focus not on the perfectibility of life, but on the lack of definable disease.[95]

But not everyone is "partly sick"; there is one who is perfect. In spite of our depraved nature, health does not lose value, as Frances suggests, if Jesus Christ is perfect as Scripture claims. But Frances is correct in stating how unattainable perfection is for fallen humanity. This reality is precisely why God's grace is so vital to being restored into the image of Christ and having our minds renewed—mankind's only means of being made perfect. It is not of works, merit, or a pill that man can obtain perfection, but by God's grace through faith in the completed work of Christ accomplished at the cross (Ephesians 2:8-10). From the biblical and eternal perspective, normalcy is not purely hypothetical: it was once experienced by Adam and Eve prior to the fall, was again exemplified in the life of Jesus Christ, and will someday be experienced by anyone who receives eternal life through the salvation provided by Jesus Christ. The way to perfection begins with a person changing their mind away from self-absorption and self-trust and toward God—what Scripture calls repentance. Though the process begins and progresses in

---

[95] Ibid.

this life, the completion will not occur until after death when true believers are fully made perfect.

      Jesus lived a perfect life and then died to pay the legal price of our sin against God. His death makes it possible for mankind to be saved from the guilt of their sin and to be changed to be like the perfect man, Jesus Christ. Colossians 1 states,

> Giving thanks to the Father, who has qualified you to share in the inheritance of the saints in light. He has delivered us from the domain of darkness and transferred us to the kingdom of his beloved Son, in whom we have redemption, the forgiveness of sins . . . . And you, who once were alienated and hostile in mind, doing evil deeds, he has now reconciled in his body of flesh by his death, in order to present you holy and blameless and above reproach before him.

Though the minds of all men and women are by nature set against Christ (and, in that sense, "mentally ill") and produce corresponding deeds or behavior, God sent His son to restore mankind to His holy/perfect likeness. When a person's spiritual nature is being transformed, so too are their behaviors. Titus 2:14 says, "Who gave himself for us to redeem us from all lawlessness and to purify for himself a people for his own possession who are zealous for good works." God sent His son Jesus so that our deceptive and sinful nature described metaphorically as mental illness could be completely remedied through the atonement and our behaviors could be made morally good. Christ, therefore, is not merely God's intended standard of normalcy for humanity, but by His perfection and atoning work, He is the only one who could provide and distribute the remedy. He is the only great physician who can heal us in every way. While this healing will not be completed or fully experienced until heaven, those who place their faith in Jesus Christ as their authority and remedy are becoming new people and experiencing mental, emotional, and behavioral transformation (2 Corinthians 5:17). Romans 12:1-2 states,

> I appeal to you therefore, brothers, by the mercies of God, to present your bodies as a living sacrifice [behavior], holy and acceptable to God, which is your spiritual worship. Do not be conformed to this world, but be transformed by the renewal of your mind, that by testing you may discern what is the will of God, what is good and acceptable and perfect.

The transformation that occurs when Christ is made to be the standard of life directly transforms the mind and lifestyle to morally please the good and perfect God. Therefore, there is a real sense in which we could say that all men and women apart from the grace of God are "mentally ill" and that Jesus is the only remedy for our corrupt minds and bodies.

These biblical truths provide an entirely new perspective on normalcy. If all sin and fall far short of God's original intent for humanity, then all are abnormal in the sense of their common depraved nature and mental chaos in reference to Christ. We are all deviants from His perfect standard. In reference to each other, however, normalcy looks like mental turmoil, chaos, and frailty. People are not strong animals as evolution makes them out to be. No one enters the world in Christ's likeness, and everyone experiences the destructive nature of his or her own sin (nature), the painful consequences of the sin of others, and the harsh experiences of the world in which we live (nurture). Romans 3:23-25 declares,

> For all have sinned and fall short of the glory of God, and are justified by his grace as a gift, through the redemption that is in Christ Jesus, whom God put forward as a propitiation by his blood, to be received by faith. This was to show God's righteousness, because in his divine forbearance he had passed over former sins.

From God the Father's perspective, all are abnormal when compared to the perfect character of Christ—His standard of normalcy, and from our common perspective, the normal human condition is to be mentally ill (metaphorically speaking) and in need of mental restoration to the mind of Christ as God intended.[96]

The Bible sees everyone, not merely a select few, as entering the world in need of mental healing. McKane touches on humanity's natural state of mind and what is required through moral education to bring about order:

> The educator's task is both to tear down and to build up; he has to eradicate as well as to implant. There are elements of chaos in the mind of the youth and order has to be restored; his innate tendency is towards folly rather than wisdom, and only the *sebet musar* [discipline] will put a distance between him and folly.[97]

Chaos and disorder, not mental health, are the natural conditions of every person's mind, and regeneration and restoration are the remedies to restore order. The only mental order that is restorative and healing is Christ's work on the cross that can be received by grace through faith.

The New Testament often uses the terms and ideas of *unrighteous* and *righteous* to establish man's position apart from Christ (Mk 2:17), and in the Old Testament, *foolish*[98] and *wise* are used to describe man's spiritual conditions in reference to God and establish an anthropological categorization of human mindsets, emotions, desires, and behavior. Secular ideology of course does not accept this system of categorization, so it creates its own construct to explain some of these same realities.

Scripture not only establishes human depravity directly, but it also explains it metaphorically using medicinal terms. It claims

---

[96] See appendix A for further study on a Christ-like mindset.

[97] William McKane, *Proverbs: A New Approach* (Philadelphia: Westminster, 1970), 564-65.

[98] There are three types of fools mentioned in Proverbs: the simple fool, the ordinary fool, and the scoffer. These terms do not indicated intelligence, but rather understanding and reception of God and his wisdom.

that everyone is spiritually, mentally, and morally "ill" (Jeremiah 17:9-10), and that God sent his son Jesus as the great physician into the world (Luke 5:31-32) to seek out those who are sick and call them to change their minds (Matthew 9:12-13).

This medicinal metaphor that reveals our incurable and common spiritual/mental condition is used throughout the Old and New Testaments (e.g., Isaiah 30:26; Jeremiah 30:12-17; Hosea 6:1). Whereas Scripture uses heart sickness or mental illness metaphorically, the secular construct of mental illness literalizes the metaphor. However, Szasz warns:

> Analogies and metaphors may be useful explanatory devices or misleading similes. In no case can an imagined or hypothesized entity be evidence of its existence as a real or physical entity.[99]

This reality is also why pastors rather than physicians cared for people's souls and their mental anguish throughout history (until the popularization of the Darwinian theory).[100] In accordance with this biblical understanding, one must conclude that in God's estimation every person is mentally ill (metaphorically) and in need of the Great Physician. Renowned secular psychiatrist Harry Stack Sullivan once said about his approach to psychiatry, "We shall assume that everyone is much more simply human than otherwise."[101] In the end, we are not so different from one another: we share the same desperate need to be restored to the image of Christ—the only true standard of perfection.

---

[99] Thomas Szasz, *Psychiatry*, 50.

[100] Szasz, *Myth of Psychotherapy*, 25-26.

[101] Harry Stack Sullivan, *Interpersonal Theory of Psychiatry* (New York: W.W. Norton Company, 1953), 32.

CHAPTER 2 – CREATING MENTAL ILLNESS

Not only is establishing normalcy of the upmost importance in understanding human abnormalities, but so also is establishing who has the right or authority to determine this standard and create a construct of mental illness. Through its ideology, classification system, medical advantage, and physicians, psychiatry—specifically the APA—has positioned itself as the current authority over mental health and is largely responsible for creating the current construct of mental illness.[102] But this place of authority should not be assumed or remain unchallenged. Accordingly, the history of psychiatry, its construct of mental illness, and especially the presuppositional worldview which enables its existence, must be carefully examined.

It is important to establish at the outset that assigning different names to the same personality characteristics, behavioral, emotional, or non-physical problems does not imply that observations and valid concerns are denied nor does it mean that such nomenclature validates attached theories.[103] In other words, the examination or rejection of the theories of modern psychiatry does not equal a denial of mental, emotional, or behavioral problems. For example, one can reject Freud's construct of psychoanalysis and instead accept the current construct. Those who reject Freud's system are not suggesting

---

[102] Scull, *Madness in Civilization*, 11.

[103] David Powlison, "Is the Adonis Complex in Your Bible?" *Journal of Biblical Counseling* 22, no. 2 (2004): 42–58

that real problems are non-existent. The discussion of mental illness, then, is not a question of whether or not someone has genuine problems; it is a matter of properly recognizing and defining the foundational problems and true causes and providing valid remedies.

A Brief History

The current paradigm of mental illness was born in Germany in the late 1800s and thereafter began to flourish in the United States. In 1896 after visiting the German psychiatrist Emil Kraepelin and learning of his new "biological psychiatry," Adolf Meyer returned to the United States and brought with him Kraepelin's construct of mental illness. While Sigmund Freud's construct of psychoanalysis would supplant Kraepelin's brain-dysfunction theory until the 1950s, Kraepelin's construct would eventually win out and become the basis of the current mental health system.

In 1946 the National Institute of Mental Health (NIMH) was established by President Harry Truman. Truman once stated,

> Never have we had a more pressing need for experts in human engineering. The greatest prerequisite for peace must be sanity, which permits clear thinking on the part of all citizens. We must continue to look to experts in the field of psychiatry and other mental science for guidance.[104]

In order to pursue "human engineering," Truman authorized the "National Mental Health Act" intended to "conduct research into the mind, brain, and behavior."[105] This legislation was a response to the many mental problems that veterans faced after

---

[104] Harry Truman quoted by Lieberman, *Shrinks*, 75.

[105] "Timeline: Treatments for Mental Illness," http://www.pbs.org/wgbh/amex/nash/timeline/.

fighting World War II.[106] Yet it also was intended to provide social guidance from "psychiatry and other mental sciences." Not long after in 1952, the American Psychiatric Association (APA) published its first *Diagnostic and Statistical Manual of Disorders (DSM)*,[107] which quickly became the secular bible for describing and categorizing human behavior under various labels.[108] Still today, most of secular psychology considers the *DSM* "the authority over our inner lives"[109] and claims it contains "some of the most rigorous and most empirically derived criteria ever available in the history of clinical diagnosis."[110]

A Claim of Authority

Today, the *DSM* (along with the APA who owns and publishes the book)[111] controls and maintains the secular construct of mental illness, and it is the primary tool that the APA claims enables their authority over moral and social issues. More specifically, the members of the APA claim it is the rigorous definitions found in the *DSM* which empower them. The former president-elect of the APA, Jeffrey Lieberman, remarks,

---

[106] "About Pediatric Bipolar Disorder (Timeline)," http://www.thebalancedmind.org/learn/library/about-pediatric-bipolar-disorder-timeline-english.

[107] Frances, *Saving Normal*, 61.

[108] Lieberman, *Shrinks*, 130.

[109] Greenberg, *Book of Woe*, 8.

[110] Barkley, *ADHD*, 14.

[111] Edward Shorter, *A History of Psychiatry: From the Era of the Asylum to the Age of the Prozac* (New York: John Wiley & Sons, 1997), 289.

> This authoritative compendium of all known mental illnesses is known as the Bible of Psychiatry [*DSM*], and for good reason—each and every hallowed diagnosis of psychiatry is inscribed within its pages. *What you may not realize is that the DSM might just be the most influential book written in the past century.* Its contents directly affect how tens of millions of people work, learn, and live—and whether they go to jail. It serves as a career manual for millions of mental health professionals including psychiatrists, psychologists, social workers, and psychiatric nurses. It dictates the payment of hundreds of billions of dollars to hospitals, physicians, pharmacies, and laboratories by Medicare, Medicaid, and private insurance companies. . . . But the manual's greatest impact is on the lives of tens of millions of men and women who long for relief from the anguish of mental disorder, since first and foremost, *the book precisely defines every known mental illness. It is these detailed definitions that empower the DSM's unparalleled medical influence over society* [emphasis added].[112]

Chair of the *DSM-IV*, Dr. Allen Frances notes the same:

> The bad news that we can't develop a useful definition for the general concept "mental disorder" is balanced by the very good news that we can *quite easily define each one of the specific mental disorders*. The method, introduced by DSM-III in 1980, is simple and effective. The description of each DSM disorder is accompanied by a criteria set that lists *in fairly precise terms* which symptoms define it, how many must be present, and their required duration [emphasis added].[113]

In these influential men's views, the nomenclature and "precise and detailed definitions" found in the *DSM* enable psychiatry to control and influence society in a profound way. In other words, they claim to have meticulously studied, discovered, and explained true human nature and genuine problems. While they claim that their authority hinges on "precise definitions" found in the *DSM*—which they personally presided over, the *DSM* itself reveals that the definitions of mental illness that it contains are neither exact nor even encompassing. It states,

> The symptoms contained in the respective *diagnostic criteria sets do not constitute comprehensive definitions* of underlying disorders, which encompass cognitive, emotional, behavioral, and physiological processes that are far more complex than can be described in these brief summaries. *Rather, they are intended to summarize* characteristic

---

[112] Lieberman, *Shrinks*, 87-88.

[113] Frances, *Saving Normal*, 23.

> syndromes of signs and symptoms that point to an underlying disorder with a characteristic developmental history, biological and environmental risk factors, neuropsychological and physiological correlates, and typical clinical course [emphasis added].[114]

Dr. Lieberman claims that psychiatry must be granted the rightful position of authority over society because of its unique ability to precisely define and explain anthropology. But as his work overseeing the *DSM-5* reveals, the definitions and constructs that psychiatry offers are imprecise and simply incomprehensive summaries. According to Lieberman's logic, then, secularists should not have authority over society when it comes to social constructs of anthropology and specifically of the human mind, emotions, behavior, and desires.

While Frances suggests that the *DSM* definitions are precise, he later admits,

> We saw *DSM-IV* as a guidebook, not a bible—*a collection of temporarily useful diagnostic constructs, not a catalog of "real" diseases* [emphasis added]. We tried to make this abundantly clear in the introduction to *DSM-IV* and at greater length in the *DSM-IV* Guidebook. Unfortunately, I am not sure anyone ever reads the introduction, and I know that few people have read the Guidebook. People shouldn't worship the *DSM* categories, but it does make you a better clinician to know them.[115]

Such statements underscore the little known but significant fact that the *DSM*'s "temporarily useful diagnostic constructs"[116] of mental illness were not intended to be worshiped or viewed as medical dogma. In fact, as Frances states, the proposed disorders it contains should not be considered diseases. Yet, unfortunately, the *DSM* is highly regarded as objective science and its labels as real indications of illness by much of society.

---

[114] APA, *DSM-5*, 19.

[115] Frances, *Saving Normal*, 73.

[116] Ibid.

Although the *DSM* offers a standardized classification system for the secular construct and presents it as the standard of authority, the book is not without controversy even among psychiatrists. For example, most view the *DSM* as reliable, the authority on psychopathology and "the Bible of psychology,"[117] but in 2013 the National Institute of Mental Health (NIMH) sent a shockwave through the mental health community when it stated that the *DSM* is, in fact, not scientifically founded and is merely "a dictionary, creating a set of labels and defining each."[118] Although this statement undermines the very authority that sustains much of its own acceptance,[119] the NIMH still attempts to hold on to the labeling system and unproven paradigm and to establish its own authority in the mental health field.[120] Others such as Dr. Francis Mondimore, also note the *DSM's* limitations and problems:

---

[117] Grossman, *On Killing*, 76.

[118] Thomas Insel, "Transforming Diagnosis," http://www.nimh.nih.gov/about/director/2013/transforming-diagnosis.shtml.

[119] The *DSM* is now fully owned by the American Psychiatric Association — a point of contention for many psychologists who still hold to psychotherapy as the only viable approach to mental illness and reject Kraepelinian theory. Still today, there is a division within the secular paradigm of those who side with Sigmund Freud and those who side with Emil Kraepelin (Lieberman, *Shrinks*, 70).

[120] The American Psychological Association seeks to replace the *DSM* with the *International Classification of Diseases* (ICD) — owned and controlled by the World Health Organization (WHO). But even the *ICD* owes its existence to the *DSM*. "'The American Psychiatric Association can really be credited with a revolution in psychiatric nosology with the publication of *DSM-III* by introducing a descriptive nosological system based on co-occurring clusters of symptoms,' said WHO psychologist Geoffrey Reed" (American Psychology Association, "ICD vs. DSM" *Monitor on Psychology* 40, no. 9 [Oct 2009]: 63). See also Mark Hubble, Barry Duncan, and Scott Miller, *The Heart and Soul of Change: What Works in Therapy* (Washington, DC: American Psychological Association, 1999), 437-38.

There are problems with the *DSM*, however, and many experts have been extremely critical of it. The *DSM* is essentially a collection of checklists of symptoms for each diagnostic category and is not based on an understanding of the causes of emotional problems. This might seem like quibbling academic question at first, but it's not.[121]

He goes on to say,

Just as the range of normal experiences and behaviors is enormous, so is the range (and complexity) of abnormal mental experiences and behaviors; they cannot be contained in any one book and certainly cannot all be described in a few dozen diagnostic categories.[122]

Likewise, the American Psychological Association writes about the *DSM*,

The *DSM*, in spite of continuing to be plagued by poor reliability and validity and having absolutely no predictive power in terms of treatment outcome, is now a fixed part of most graduate training programs and a prominent feature of the whole empirically validated treatment movement. . . . The development of valid and reliable alternatives to the empirically bankrupt approaches sponsored by the American Psychiatric Association [the *DSM*] is possible using the very same body of research that psychologists have been instrumental in creating.[123]

The problems with the *DSM* are so extensive that Dr. Frances admits with regret the harmful effects of the various *DSMs* in which he played a major role:

On the negative side: Our changes [to the *DSM-IV*] contributed directly to the false epidemics of autistic, attention deficit, and adult bipolar disorder; we did nothing to prevent the overdiagnosis (sic) of several other disorders that have been puffed up by the drug companies; and our one outright mistake was a disaster, a sloppily worded paraphilia section that has allowed the widespread unconstitutional abuse of involuntary psychiatric hospitalization . . . . Now I wish we had done more to save normal and reduce the ease with which the drug companies were able to sell sickness. . . . The *DSMs* have a mixed record. They have served an extremely valuable function in improving the reliability of psychiatric diagnosis and in

---

[121] Francis Mark Mondimore, *Bipolar Disorder: A Guide for Patients and Families*, 3rd ed. (Baltimore: Johns Hopkins University Press, 2014), 55.

[122] Ibid., 57.

[123] Mark A. Hubble, Barry L. Duncan, and Scott D. Miller, *The Heart and Soul of Change: What Works in Therapy* (Washington, DC: American Psychological Association, 1999), 437-38.

> encouraging a revolution in psychiatric research. But they have also had the very harmful unintended consequence of triggering and helping to maintain a runaway diagnostic inflation that threatens normal and results in massive overtreatment with psychiatric medication.[124]

Statements such as these reveal that the scientific dogma of the modern mental health community is, in fact, only faith in a poorly constructed system established from a secular worldview. Though insiders, such as the aforementioned, expose the subjectivity, harmful effects, and lack of scientific validity of the *DSM*, it remains foundational to the current secular theories of mental illness, and it is still considered by most to be the authority for defining, diagnosing, categorizing, and treating mental illnesses.

In spite of its popularity and wide acceptance, the *DSM* is simply not scientifically defensible.[125] It remains the standard,[126] however, because many professionals insist that it provides "an essential stop-gap measure that is socially needed until the etiology [causes] of psychiatric disorders are revealed."[127] Secularists claim that the book provides a necessary consensus on what should be considered abnormal, but Dr. Bentall disagrees: "What is clear is that the apparent consensus created by the *DSM* system is illusory."[128] In spite of this fact, many

---

[124] Frances, *Saving Normal*, 75-76.

[125] Greenberg, *Book of Woe*, 20-21.

[126] "In the U.S., mental disorders are diagnosed based on the *Diagnostic and Statistical Manual of Mental Disorders*," (National Institute of Mental Health, "The Numbers Count: Mental Disorders in America," http://www.nimh.nih.gov/health/publications/the-numbers-count-mental-disorders-in-america/index.shtml).

[127] Jaak Panksepp, ed., *Textbook of Biological Psychiatry* (New York: John Wiley and Sons, 2004), 18.

[128] Bentall, *Madness Explained*, 65.

psychiatrists, like Professor Jerold Maxmen of Columbia University, claim that through the *DSM* "the ascendance of scientific psychiatry became official . . . the old [psychoanalytical] psychiatry derives from theory, the new psychiatry from fact."[129] Within the secular construct, the *DSM* is the accepted scientific authority — the lesser of all available evils — until actual facts can be realized.

This point, however, demands further clarity: the secular construct of mental illness, which created categories and labels for common human behavior, mindsets, and emotions, did not create preexisting desires, mindsets, emotions, and behaviors. In other words, the *DSM* does not introduce any new idea, identify new behavior, or even provide new explanations for causes of behavior. Instead, it simply provides new medicalized labels to describe and categorize human impairment and distress. Former professor of psychiatry at Duke University, Allen Frances explains, "The ancient shaman had different names and explanations — but these worked almost as well for him as current names and explanations work for the modern shrink."[130] All approaches to the mind and any idea of mental illness recognize that these characteristics of human beings, no matter how they are labeled, have existed throughout history and across all cultures.

Likewise, the current system represents a shift in social thinking and a clear redefining of mental illness. Originally, in the 1800s, psychiatrists were a specialized group of doctors

---

[129] Jarold Maxmen, *The New Psychiatrists* (New York: New American Library, 1985), 31, 35.

[130] Frances, *Saving Normal*, 36.

trained to handle "idiocy/insanity."[131] Their practice was confined to psychiatric wards,[132] and their classification system was only intended "as a statistical classification of institutionalized mental patients."[133] Furthermore, their practice was limited to dealing primarily with only two disorders: schizophrenia and bipolar disorders. Modern psychiatrists, however, now treat the general public for a wide variety of issues. In fact, Dr. Frances comments on the irrational process by which behaviors, mindsets, and emotions are now considered to be abnormalities and categories listed in the *DSM*. He explains,

> The mental disorders included in *DSM-5* have not gained their official status through any rational process of elimination. They made it into the system and have survived because of practical necessity, historical accident, gradual accretion, precedent, and inertia—not because they met some independent set of abstract and universal definitional criteria. No surprise then that the *DSM* disorders are something of a hodgepodge, not internally consistent or mutually exclusive.[134]

What was once only two constructs of madness during Kraepelin and Freud's day now amounts to hundreds of psychiatric labels for common life experiences and reactions.

The change in quantity of alleged disorders and labels directly corresponds to the acceptance of Freud's theory of psychoanalysis in the late 1800s/early 1900s and the later acceptance of Kraepelin's brain-dysfunction theory in the early 1950s. With these two men established as authorities, a new

---

[131] "*DSM*: History of the Manual," http://www.psychiatry.org/practice/dsm/dsm-history-of-the-manual.

[132] Joseph Pierre, "A Mad World," March 19, 2014, http://aeon.co/magazine/psychology/have-psychiatrists-lost-perspective-on-mental-illness/.

[133] APA, *DSM-5*, 6.

[134] Frances, *Saving Normal*, 17.

definition of mental illness emerged, and the psychiatrist's role and practice were reinvented:

> Now, for the first time in psychiatry's inglorious history, Freud's remarkable new therapy of psychoanalysis granted alienists the opportunity to establish office-based practices of their own. Whether a devotee of Freud, Adler, Jung, or Rank, the psychoanalyst could treat wealthy patients with minor mental maladies in the civil environs of a comfortably appointed drawing room. *Of course embracing psychoanalysis meant embracing a radical redefinition of mental illness* [emphasis added]. Previously, the boundary between sick and healthy was drawn between those who needed to be institutionalized and those who did not need to be institutionalized. To be mentally ill meant one was seriously mentally ill.[135]

Historian Edward Short notes,

> By the 1970s, the progress of science within psychiatry would dim the light on this scenario, marginalizing psychoanalysis within the discipline of psychiatry as a whole. In retrospect, Freud's psychoanalysis appears as a pause in the evolution of biological approaches to brain and mind rather than as the culminating event in the history of psychiatry. Yet it was a pause of enormous consequence for psychiatry. Freud's psychoanalysis offered psychiatrists a way out of the asylum. The practice of depth psychology, based on Freud's views, permitted psychiatrists for the first time in history to establish themselves as an office-based specialty and to wrest psychotherapy from the neurologists.[136]

With Freud's psychoanalytic theory, the idea of mental illness was reinvented and redefined.

Furthermore, the transfer of authority (in the 1950s and 1960s) from the hands of psychologists and neurologists into the governing system of psychiatrists enabled the introduction of countless new so-called illnesses that defined many normal people as disordered and enabled psychiatrists to claim their position as legitimate practitioners of all the soul's woes. Secular psychiatrist, Bessel van der Kolk remarks,

> Now a new paradigm was emerging: Anger, lust, pride, greed, avarice, and sloth—as well as all the other problems we humans have always struggled to manage—were recast as "disorders" that

---

[135] Lieberman, *Shrinks*, 72.

[136] Shorter, *History of Psychiatry*, 145.

> could be fixed by the administration of appropriate chemicals. Many psychiatrists were relieved and delighted to become "real scientists," just like their med school classmates who had laboratories, animal experiments, expensive equipment, and complicated diagnostic tests, and set aside the wooly-headed theories of philosophers like Freud and Jung.[137]

This asserted power gave psychiatrists and psychologists the privilege to name and control human struggles and moral character according to their humanistic ideologies. But psychiatrists have not merely asserted their authority by creating definitions, they have also gained authority, acceptance, and control by adding to their construct new labels that redefined normalcy as abnormality. Simply by categorizing and labeling impairing or undesirable human behavior with medical sounding terminology, secularists have managed to convince many that these newly created constructs are actually diseases.

Renaming or branding something often establishes the author as the authority and suggests dominion. Other times labeling or renaming is merely an attempt to gain power. Whereas God gave the privilege to Adam to name the animals in the Garden of Eden (Genesis 1:26; 2:19-20), psychiatry has assumed its right to rename common human behavior, desires, emotions, and mindsets (e.g., sorrow and hopelessness became depression). Dr. Szasz explains the power of creating labels and definitions:

> Definitions, especially the power to construct definitions and to impose them on others, are of great importance in all aspects of human life. In psychiatry and psychotherapy, because these disciplines deal with human relations and with the influence of persons and groups on one another, how words are used is extremely important.[138]

---

[137] Van der Kolk, *The Body Keeps the Score*, 27.

[138] Szasz, *Myth of Psychotherapy*, 4.

He goes on to write that some rhetoricians use language to establish their authority and assert power.[139] In a similar manner, Dr. Greenberg remarks,

> Psychiatry's appeal is not just about the possibility of cure, which is why the profession continues to flourish even when it cures nothing and relieves symptoms only haphazardly. It's in the naming itself. . . . Give a name to suffering, perhaps the most immediate reminder of our insignificance and powerlessness, and suddenly it bears the trace of the human. It becomes part of our story. It is redeemed.[140]

Creating new nomenclature and constructs to describe common or normal human behavior, mindsets, and emotions (albeit impairing) often establishes a new authority.[141] However, simply relabeling and categorizing human behavior, mindsets, and emotions should not grant authority since categorizing and labeling is normal human nature. Dr. Allen Frances explains,

> Man is the naming animal — we can't stop ourselves from putting a label on everything in sight. This has been our special gift, and sometimes our curse, ever since Genesis, when Adam established his dominion over the plants and animals by the simple act of naming them. Diagnostic exuberance is built into our DNA. We have a strong need to identify patterns — to distinguish lion from lamb, food from poison, friend from foe.[142]

Psychiatrist Lawrie Reznek understands how a suggested theory or a label can quickly be transformed into a mental illness by the established authority. He writes,

> Suppose psychiatrists drafting the *DSM V* argue that prejudice should be classified as a disease called Prejudice Disorder (PD). They argue that a prejudiced person is the victim of a deep-seated sense of inferiority such that his ego is unable to tolerate the idea that others are his equal. He has to ensure that they are inferior. This need and fear, supposedly, are severe enough to paralyze his reason so that he

---

[139] Ibid., 20.

[140] Greenberg, *Book of Woe*, 14.

[141] Of course most clinicians deny that their labels encroach on normalcy (Pierre, "A Mad World") .

[142] Frances, *Saving Normal*, 35.

> is unable to correct his views of the minority group against whom he is prejudiced. If Jock suffers from PD, his ignorance will satisfy the rules of exculpatory ignorance.[143]

The ease with which alleged disorders can be created is alarming. In his book, *Saving Normal*, Dr. Frances remarks on the many disorders proposed for the latest version of the *DSM* (5), yet were at the last minute rejected with the change of leadership. But he also insists that two-thirds of the new labels that were added to the *DSM-5* are bogus and detrimental to society:

> *DSM-5* has just been published — not a happy moment in the history of psychiatry or for me personally. It risks turning diagnostic inflation into hyperinflation — further cheapening the currency of psychiatric diagnosis and unleashing a wave of new false epidemics.[144]

Dr. Frances goes on to mention some of the proposed disorders: rape, temper-tantrums, promiscuity, and somatic symptom disorder (a mental illness allegedly caused by a valid diseases such as cancer).[145] For psychiatrists, the list seems endless with new labels that can be assigned to common impairments.

Whether admitted or not, psychiatric labels are powerful, and they can change one's perspective of life and self. One of the newest suggested labels, which comes from the self-proclaimed authority on ADHD Russell Barkley is "Sluggish Cognitive Tempo." Keith McBurnett quoted by Schwarz remarks,

> These children are not the ones giving adults much trouble, so they're easy to miss. . . . They're the day dreamy ones, the ones with work that's not turned in, leaving names off of papers or skipping questions, things like that, that impinge on grades or performance.

---

[143] Reznek, *Evil or Ill*, 207.

[144] Frances, *Saving Normal*, 170.

[145] Ibid., 194.

> So anything we can do to understand what's going on with these kids is a good thing.[146]

But Dr. Allen Frances offers a different perspective:

> I have no doubt there are kids who meet the criteria for this thing [SCT], but nothing is more irrelevant.... The enthusiasts here are thinking of missed patients. What about the mislabeled kids who are called patients when there's nothing wrong with them? They are not considering what is happening in the real world.[147]

Another example of this misguided labeling is the *DSM-5* construct of *encopresis* ("repeated passage of feces into inappropriate places [e.g., clothing, floor], whether involuntary or intentional")[148] which transforms a normal but undesirable childish behavior into an abnormality/illness. Many parents become deceived into thinking their children are abnormal in reference to other children. When in truth, these children are simply impaired or distressed humans like the rest of us.

Although these psychiatric labels are said to be helpful and necessary, many times their labels cause further damage[149] and by nature create the very stigma mental health professionals claim they wish to eliminate. In fact, being labeled as abnormal in itself stigmatizes individuals since it unjustly delineates people into subjective groups. Herein rests one of the problems the secular paradigm cannot escape: to be diagnosed as mentally ill is to be categorized as abnormal. Dr. Frances explains:

---

[146] Allen Schwarz, "Idea of New Attention Disorder Spurs Research, and Debate," *New York Times* (April 11, 2014), http://www.nytimes.com/2014/04/12/health/idea-of-new-attention-disorder-spurs-research-and-debate.html?emc=eta1&_r=2&utm_source=January+2015&utm_campaign=Constant+Contact&utm_medium=email.

[147] Ibid.

[148] APA, *DSM-5*, 357.

[149] Frances, *Saving Normal*, 252.

Being "normal" and fitting in with the pack are a key to survival. Evolution has wired into human nature an uncharitable wariness and lack of compassion for those who are different and don't satisfy tribal standards. Having a mental disorder label "marks" someone in ways that can cause much secondary harm.[150]

Dr. Breggin also remarks of how labels "mark" or stigmatize as it too often applies to children:

> Psychiatric labeling inflicts additional humiliation and injury on already damaged children. It can rob them of all self-esteem, shatter their identity among their peers, and relegate them to inferior status in the eyes of parents and teachers. Often the stigma remains for a lifetime.[151]

Similarly, Dr. Frances remarks of the stigma commonly associated with the label of Childhood Bipolar Disorder (CBD):

> CBD also carries considerable stigma, implying that the child will have a lifelong illness requiring lifetime treatment. The diagnosis can distort a person's life narrative, cutting off hopes of otherwise achievable ambitions, and also may reduce a sense of control over, and responsibility for, undesirable behavior.... The CBD fad is the most shameful episode in my forty-five years of observing psychiatry. The widespread use of dangerous medicine to treat a fake diagnosis constitutes a vast public health experiment with no informed consent.[152]

Even the highly respected Karl Menninger once wrote to fellow psychiatrist Thomas Szasz,

> I think I understand better what has disturbed you these years and, in fact, it disturbs me, too, now. We don't like the situation that prevails whereby a fellow human being is put aside, outcast as it were, ignored, labeled and said to be "sick in his mind."[153]

Psychiatric labels that categorize people as abnormal for behaving normally are damaging and isolate people with mental

---

[150] Ibid., 109.

[151] Breggin, *Toxic Psychiatry*, 291.

[152] Frances, *Saving Normal*, 146.

[153] Karl Menninger, Reading Notes, *Bulletin of the Menninger Clinic*, 53, no. 4 (July 1989): 350-52. See also http://www.szasz.com/menninger.html.

and emotional needs from genuine help they so desperately need. While there is a tremendous effort on the part of secularists to remove the stigma of mental illness, the stigma exists not because of society's perception, but because the very nature of the current construct of mental illness creates it.

Labels also have another benefit for those who create them. Roy Porter explains:

> Setting the sick apart sustains the fantasy that we are whole. Disease diagnosis thus constitutes a powerful classificatory tool, and medicine contributes its fair share to the stigmatizing enterprise. Amongst those scapegoated and anathematized by means of this cognitive apartheid, the 'insane' have, of course, been conspicuous.[154]

What Porter rightly expresses is that a system that ostracizes, labels, and scapegoats others best serves those who have the authority to do so. Labeling not only stigmatizes the one labeled, it affords those in authority who are granted the privilege to assign labels a false sense of security that they are okay while others are not.

Furthermore, labels can create mental turmoil where none existed before and cause the one labeled to fulfill the expected role of the diagnosis. Dr. Frances explains,

> Labels can also create self-fulfilling prophecies. If you are told you are sick, you feel and act sick, and others treat you as if you are sick. The sick role can be enormously useful when someone truly is sick and needs respite and care. But the sick role can be extremely destructive when it reduces expectations, truncates ambitions, and results in a loss of personal responsibility.[155]

Psychiatric labels too often establish a new identity for the one labeled. In fact, many who are diagnosed begin to find their identity in their new label and alleged disease over any other characteristic they possess, commonly stating that "I am bipolar,

---

[154] Porter, *Madness*, 63.

[155] Frances, *Saving Normal*, 109.

schizophrenic, or depressed." Mental health professionals try to keep the mindsets, emotions, and behaviors represented in psychiatric diagnoses from being perceived as character issues, yet those who are categorized according to psychiatric labels often identify their own character by such nomenclature. Still others are self-diagnosing and creating a new type of self-fulfillment based on the common knowledge of psychiatric labels.[156] Psychiatrists Til Wykes and Felicity Callard explain:

> Both the meanings that people attach to the feelings and behaviours they are experiencing, as well as societally sanctioned explanations for these feelings and behaviours play an important role in shaping people's ways of embodying a psychiatric diagnosis. Consider, for example, the recent report of a new phenomenon: patients in Britain approaching psychiatrists with self-identified bipolar disorder. This suggests that, despite the ongoing and pervasive stigma attached to a "severe mental illness" diagnosis, individuals are beginning to understand as well as self-describe some of their own patterns of behaviour and emotional variability as a list of symptoms that – when gathered together – make them people "with bipolar". It is likely, then, that the introduction of new diagnostic categories to *DSM-5* will play an important – though as yet not fully understood or anticipated – part in reshaping the ways in which both individuals as well as society conceptualize both mental distress and "patienthood".[157]

Labels are sometimes helpful, but more often than not they are powerful tools to gain authority, to stigmatize people, and to change beliefs, lifestyles, and even identities.

---

[156] Diana Chan and Lester Sireling, "I want to be bipolar": A New Phenomenon, *Psychiatrist*, 34, no. 3 (March 1, 2010); 103–105.

[157] Wykes and Callard, "Diagnosis."

CHAPTER 3 – DEFINING MENTAL ILLNESS

In order to understand the current construct of mental illness, it is important to learn about the men largely responsible for the construct and the *DSM*. Though they are no longer prominent, each of them made significant contributions to the public perception of mental illness and its treatment.

Emil Kraepelin

One of the most important men in psychiatry's brief history and the man most responsible for the current construct of mental illness was German psychiatrist, outspoken supporter of social Darwinism, and promoter of racial hygiene,[158] Emil Kraepelin. Kraepelin is considered by the psychiatric community to be the founder of modern psychiatry as well as the father of psychopharmacology[159] and psychiatric genetics.[160] One of his most significant works, *Compendium der Psychiatrie*, published in 1883, "would have near-revolutionary impact on the theory of psychiatry."[161] In it, he proposed that mental illness was a branch of science that should be practiced through the scientific processes of observation and experimentation and not from a faith-based or religious standpoint as it had been approached

---

[158] Kraepelin's genetic theories and system of psychiatry would eventually lead to the Jewish Holocaust. "Emil Kraepelin," http://en.wikipedia.org/wiki/Emil_Kraepelin.

[159] Valenstein, *Blaming the Brain*, 10.

[160] "Emil Kraepelin (1856-1926)," http://www.goodtherapy.org/famous-psychologists/emil-kraepelin.html. See also "Emil Kraepelin (1856-1926)," http://www.sciencemuseum.org.uk/broughttolife/people/emilkraepelin.aspx.

[161] Bentall, *Madness Explained*, 10.

throughout most of history.[162] His proposed classification system of human behavior would years later become the foundation to the current secular construct and shape the modern *DSM*[163] and the *International Classification of Diseases (ICD)*:[164]

> Kraepelin's original taxonomy described the outlines of major psychiatric categories still accepted today. His textbooks had clear descriptions of syndromes that we now recognize as schizophrenia, various phobias, depression, and anxiety disorders with their links to obsessions and compulsions. The modern standard classification schemes, ever since the *DSM*-1 of 1951, have clearly followed the Kraepelinian outline.[165]

Kraepelin's degrees in both neurology and psychology, along with his faith in Darwinian theory, led him to suggest new conclusions about anthropology and social engineering; thus, the foundation for the modern concept of biological psychiatry was first conceived. Though they often disagreed, both Kraepelin and Sigmund Freud believed that the scientific concept of physiological disease should somehow be applied to the mind.[166]

Furthermore, both Freud and Kraepelin held to the deterministic view which teaches that man cannot help who he is or what he does, but that he is a product of his nurture and/or brain and genetics (nature). For Freud, nature and nurture meant past subconscious desires and outworking relationships (his psychoanalytic theory).[167] Whereas for Kraepelin, nurture was not as much a point of concern as was the nature of humanity.

---

[162] Szasz, *Myth of Psychotherapy*, 25.

[163] Coville, Costello, and Rouke, *Abnormal Psychology*, 8-9.

[164] Frances, *Saving Normal*, 59. See also, Shorter, *History of Psychiatry*, 106.

[165] Panksepp, *Biological Psychiatry*, 17.

[166] Lieberman, *Shrinks*, 97.

[167] Szasz, *Myth of Psychotherapy*, 6-7.

Kraepelin's Darwinian beliefs led him to view human nature materialistically, rejecting the idea that people consist of a spiritual and physical nature. The idea of human nature, to him, meant that the brain, genetics, chemicals, and even the mind were all material matters that science could study. Thus Kraepelin's evolutionary beliefs and theory of mental illness established the brain-dysfunction theory which is still held as fact today. Though never proved, the brain-dysfunction theory has become so engrained in modern psychiatric thinking that many secularists refuse to question it.[168] This new focus on biology and theories about the mind-brain connection are why this era in German psychiatric history is known as "the age of the first biological psychiatry."[169] Ironically, Emil Kraepelin was uninterested in studying the brain's biology and instead focused on his brain-dysfunction theory, which attempted to reduce the mind to merely a function of the brain.[170]

While Freud's construct of psychoanalysis fell by the wayside in the early 1950s, Kraepelin's proposed theory is still the foundation of the construct of mental illness today. The historian Edward Shorter remarks, "It is Kraepelin, not Freud, who is the central figure in the history of psychiatry."[171] Even after his death, mental health professionals believed that "Kraepelin could save psychiatry."[172] The belief is still prevalent today as observed in the ongoing acceptance of Kraepelin's original theory. Richard Bentall notes four reasons why

---

[168] Bentall, *Madness Explained*, 42.

[169] Shorter, *History of Psychiatry*, 69-81.

[170] Ibid., 300. This point will be developed further in volume 3.

[171] Ibid., 100.

[172] Ibid., 130.

Kraepelin remains the father of the current construct: (1) modern textbooks are organized according to Kraepelin's paradigm, (2) the APA and the World Health Organization (WHO) both organize their classification system based on Kraepelin's assumptions about the nature of normalcy and madness, (3) most research conducted is an attempt to prove Kraepelin's construct or is guided by his presuppositions, and (4) most clinicians employ Kraepelin's construct in their offices and with their patients.[173]

While it is important to know Kraepelin's significant role in history, it is equally important to know his worldview and outworking theory of mental illness. Kraepelin's paradigm is based on the theory that humans, including the mind/spirit, are only material, entirely products of biological evolution. The underlying philosophy behind this assertion is called *materialism* or *positivism*: "A theory that physical matter is the only or fundamental reality and that all being and processes and phenomena can be explained as manifestations or results of matter."[174] Materialism is a philosophy/anthropology that dates well before Kraepelin's time, but Kraepelin's application of it to the mind's struggles became the empowering belief system behind the current construct of mental illness.[175]

---

[173] Bentall, *Madness Explained*, 42.

[174] "Materialism," http://www.merriam-webster.com/dictionary/materialism.

[175] Some historians believe it was Hippocrates of Cos who first proposed the idea of materialism (Porter, *Madness*, 37).

Table A

The Tenets of Neo-Kraepelinian Orthodoxy

1. Psychiatry must be viewed as a distinct and valid branch of medicine.
2. Psychiatry must rely on the scientific method and change only in accordance with evolving science.
3. Biological psychiatry establishes the boundary between normal, mentally healthy people and those who are sick and need treatment.
4. Though no biological markers and no objective means may be available to make a diagnosis, *DSM* nomenclature must still be viewed as discrete illnesses and not mere speculation or myth.
5. It is the privilege and responsibility of psychiatry to define, research, treat, and specialize in human conditions deemed to be mental illness.
6. The focus of research, treatment, diagnosis, and classification of mental illnesses must be on biology, validating theories and etiological claims, and on improving reliability.
7. Utilitarianism or group consensus must be the guide to standards, labels, categorizations, and diagnoses.
8. The agreed upon classification system must be upheld and taught until a new consensus is met to replace the previous one.

To be truly "Kraepelinian," "meant that one operated within a 'medical model.'"[176] The historian Roy Porter remarks on this philosophy:

---

[176] Shorter, *History of Psychiatry*, 108. See table A, adapted from Gerald Klerman's NeoKraepelinian manifesto – Gerald L. Klerman, "The Evolution of a

Human life, in sickness and in health, was to be understood in naturalistic terms. As one of those Hippocratic texts tells us, "Men ought to know that from the brain, and from the brain only, arise our pleasures, joys, laughter, and jests, as well as our sorrows, pain, grief and tears. . . . It is the same thing which makes us mad or delirious, inspires us with dread and fear, whether by night or by day, brings sleeplessness, inopportune mistakes, aimless anxieties, absentmindedness, and acts that are contrary to habit." Medicine thus excluded the supernatural by definition.[177]

"By definition," western medicine had excluded the supernatural and thus enabled physicians alone to care for the soul. This belief in classic materialism or positivism and subsequent trust in the medical model or "disease entity"[178] approach was central to Kraepelin's theory and remains one of the foundational tenets of today's construct. As was true in Kraepelin's era in Germany, the widespread acceptance of Kraepelin's theory in America and throughout the world is largely attributable to the ever-growing acceptance of Darwinian anthropology.[179]

Kraepelin constructed his ideology on genetic purity, strict materialism, and the proposal that pharmaceuticals should be used to treat man's mental and behavioral struggles. He also claimed his theories were backed by science. Though when carefully examined, they are actually scientism (faith in the scientific process).

The modern pharmacology movement to treat alleged mental illness was likewise a creation of Kraepelin's materialistic construct. In fact, it was Kraepelin who coined the term

---

Scientific Nosology" from J.C. Shershow, *Schizophrenia: Science and Practice* (Cambridge, MA: Harvard University Press, 1978), and Bentall, *Madness Explained*, 58-63.

[177] Porter, *Madness*, 37.

[178] Ibid., 184.

[179] Lieberman, *Shrinks*, 96.

pharmacopsychology.[180] The website *Good Therapy* states of Kraepelin:

> Kraepelin was an advocate for eugenics, as he believed certain groups of people were genetically predisposed to mental disorders. . . . . Although few people are aware of his influence, Kraepelin's work is at the foundation of all diagnostic measures used in psychology today, including the American Psychiatric Association's Diagnostic and Statistical Manual of Mental Disorders (*DSM*) and the World Health Organization's International Classification of Diseases (*ICD*). Kraepelin also pioneered research in psychopharmacology.[181]

While Kraepelin's construct proposed an etiology of mental illness and a pharmacological/biological remedy, he did not see his theory as a reliable source of healing for those with mental struggles. Lieberman remarks of Kraepelin's confession before his death,

> In 1917, Emil Kraepelin captured the pervasive sense of hopelessness among clinicians when he told his colleagues, "We can rarely alter the course of mental illness. We must openly admit that the vast majority of the patients placed in our institutions are forever lost."[182]

By his own testimony, Kraepelin identified that his construct and proposed remedy of pharmacology would most likely not heal anyone from their mental despair. In fact, many psychiatrists now look upon the history of Kraepelin's system as nothing short of "disastrous."[183] Yet still, pharmaceutical companies continue to explore every possible chemical combination to reset the brain. To be fair, Kraepelin's construct was built around those who were considered to be "mad," which at that time amounted to not much more than the diagnoses of

---

[180] Valenstein, *Blaming the Brain*, 10.

[181] "Emil Kraepelin (1856-1926)," http://www.goodtherapy.org/famous-psychologists/emil-kraepelin.html.

[182] Lieberman, *Shrinks*, 153.

[183] Bentall, *Madness Explained*, 43.

schizophrenia and bipolar and any odd or unexplainable behavior. His theory, however, did not account for the current and ever-growing proposed disorders found in the *DSM*. Dr. Frances sees this disconnect as a problem:

> Kraepelin had a big blind spot—he was a hospital-based doctor who never saw an outpatient. His conception of psychiatry was formed by, and restricted to, those who were ill enough to require long-term confinement, and his classification lacked appropriate niches for most of the people who are diagnosed today.[184]

Kraepelin was not proposing a theory to heal people, but a practical anthropological theory in accordance with his Darwinian beliefs to help him both explain why people were mad and to manage those who were institutionalized and considered to be mad. For decades, psychiatry's main practice was to act as "gatekeepers" who protected society from those who were considered crazy.[185] Historically, psychiatry has been a means of social control rather than a healing branch of medicine.

Additionally, Kraepelin's construct consisted of three key elements, which are still foundational to today's accepted construct of mental illness. According to *Mental and Neurological Public Health: A Global Perspective*, the "three main features of Kraepelin's legacy"[186] are (1) a tendency to classify according to behavior rather than to search for the individual causes and remedies, (2) a firm faith in theories of eugenics or genetics with "roots . . . in Nazi Germany and the Victorian England of Galton,"[187] and (3) the reliance on biological means to treat

---

[184] Frances, *Saving Normal*, 59.

[185] Porter, *Madness*, 186.

[186] Vikram Patel et al., *Mental and Neurological Public Health: A Global Perspective* (San Diego: Academic Press, 2010), 477.

[187] Ibid., 477-78.

mental illness based on a materialistic/deterministic worldview. *Psychopathic predisposition* is the term coined by Kraepelin to reflect his deterministic views.[188] The belief that a person's brain and genetics control moral behavior and thoughts and that individuals have no say in what the brain decides is still the predominant and foundational ideology today. One psychiatrist asserts,

> The third assumption about bio-determinism also resonates strongly today in relation to treatment preferences and etiological assumptions in psychiatry.... The dominant etiological theories in psychiatry reflect bio-determinism.[189]

Kraepelin's system of diagnosis and measurements, his proposed remedy of psychotropic drugs, and his very construct, though now slightly modified, are all still foundational pillars to the secular construct of mental illness. Kraepelin is the most significant figure in the discussion of mental illness, and his belief system and outworking practices will be discussed throughout this series of books.

Sigmund Freud

Sigmund Freud is one of the most widely recognized figures in mental health, but his psychodynamic theory is not significant to the current construct. Rather, it is his propagation of materialism and determinism over spiritualism that has had the greatest impact on the current construct. This change of anthropology from viewing human beings as both spiritual (and thus moral) and physical to viewing them only as evolved matter provided the framework for how society (and many

---

[188] Shorter, *History of Psychiatry*, 106.

[189] Patel et al., *Mental and Neurological Public Health*, 478.

Christians) views and approaches the ideas surrounding mental illness:

> [Mankind] was now seen as being part of the natural order, different from non-human animals only in degree of structural complexity. This made it possible and plausible, for the first time, to treat man as an object of scientific investigation, and to conceive of the vast and varied range of human behavior, and the motivational causes from which it springs, as being amenable in principle to scientific explanation. Much of the creative work done in a whole variety of diverse scientific fields over the next century was to be inspired by, and derive sustenance from, this new world-view.[190]

Similarly Dr. Lieberman notes,

> Freud-influenced ideas became the core of virtually every medical school program in psychiatry — and, indeed, became an *all-embracing worldview* that permeated the training of every aspiring psychiatrist [emphasis added].[191]

Dr. Szasz also comments on Freud's worldview:

> Instead of believing in God, he believed in Charcot.[192] The age of medicalization had dawned. Validating fake illness as real illness, psychopathology as neuropathology, Charcot opened the floodgates. Freud proceeded to inundate the world with fake diseases, perverting the epistemology of disease and corrupting the ethics of medicine.[193]

Freud's construct of psychoanalysis is no longer relevant to the field of mental health, but the same underlying belief that a human being is strictly a biological entity and a product of evolution remains a foundational tenet of the current neo-Kraepelinian construct.

---

[190] "Sigmund Freud (1856-1939)," http://www.iep.utm.edu/freud/#H2.

[191] Lieberman, *Shrinks*, 76.

[192] Jean-Martin Charcot was a French neurologist and professor of anatomical pathology. He is also known as "the father of modern neurology."

[193] Szasz, *Psychiatry*, 22.

Robert Spitzer

Another important individual in the current secular construct is Robert Spitzer, regarded by his colleagues as the "godfather of modern psychiatric diagnosis" and the "principal author of the *Diagnostic and Statistical Manual of Disorders, 3rd Ed, (DSM-III; 1975).*"[194] Dr. Frances remarks about Spitzer,

> Without Robert Spitzer, psychiatry might have become increasingly irrelevant, drifting back to its prewar obscurity. It is rare that one man saves a profession, but psychiatry badly needed saving and Bob was a rare man.[195]

Spitzer is a highly regarded pillar in biological psychiatry, and how he saved psychiatry is key to understanding the current construct of mental illness. Drs. Herb Kutchins and Stuart Kirk (both involved in producing the *DSM-III*) write about Spitzer:

> Under Spitzer's direction, detailed instructions for making evaluations were officially adopted by the American Psychiatric Association for the first time, and claims were made that the new manual was scientifically sound. We will show that the claims made for the accuracy and scientific value of *DSM-III* and subsequent editions of the manual are questionable, but there is no doubt about the widespread acceptance of *DSM-III* and its enormous impact. . . . Not only has he identified the mental disorders of individual clients, but he also created new diagnostic categories for mental disorders. In fact, he has undoubtedly designed or refashioned more new diagnoses than any other living person in the field of mental health.[196]

When people are diagnosed with a psychiatric label, they are categorized according to Spitzer's diagnostic criteria. While Spitzer created numerous new alleged sicknesses found in the *DSM-III*, he also reinvented Kraepelin's construct of mental illness by adding new demarcations for defining normal and abnormal. Spitzer seemingly managed to do what Kraepelin had

---

[194] Kutchins and Kirk, *Making Us Crazy*, 4-5.

[195] Frances, *Saving Normal*, 62.

[196] Kutchins and Kirk, *Making us Crazy*, 5. See also Shorter, *History of Psychiatry*, 300.

originally hoped to accomplish: to turn various mental and behavioral problems into distinct physical diseases. Ed Shorter explains,

> Spitzer decided to take psychiatric diagnosis in another direction entirely, making the diagnoses as precise as possible in order to correspond to what were presumably natural disease entities. This was known as "cutting nature at the joints," and was precisely what Kraepelin had set out to do many years previously.[197]

Ironically, Spitzer's new definition of illness would be accepted as medically sound and scientific when in reality his alterations took Kraepelin's original paradigm further into the realm of subjectivity and away from validity or true science. Nonetheless, this new definition or "neo-Kraepelinian orthodoxy"[198] quickly became secular dogma. Former president-elect of the APA Dr. Lieberman writes of Spitzer's tweak of Kraepelin's construct: "It would fundamentally and irrevocably alter the medical definition of mental illness."[199] Many believe that Spitzer's reinvention of the idea of illness granted him and psychiatry unparalleled authority in matters of the mind.[200]

Additionally, Spitzer's neo-Kraepelinian ideology would marginalize all other secular constructs of mental illness (including Freud's) and establish psychiatry as the current secular authority for mental health.[201] Spitzer's alterations to Kraepelin's original theory were not only key to saving

---

[197] Shorter, *History of Psychiatry*, 300.

[198] Patel et al., *Mental and Neurological Public Health*, 477.

[199] Lieberman, *Shrinks*, 136.

[200] Bob Spitzer quoted by Alix Spiegel "The Dictionary of Disorder: How One Man Revolutionized Psychiatry," *New Yorker* (January 3, 2005), http://www.newyorker.com/magazine/2005/01/03/the-dictionary-of-disorder.

[201] Frances, *Saving Normal*, 65.

psychiatry, but they also successfully redefined common mental, emotional, and behavioral struggles in a way that the general population would accept these new ideas as diseases and brain-disorders.[202]

Although there was a task force working under Spitzer's care, it was Spitzer who conceived and oversaw the accepted neo-Kraepelinian construct in place today.[203] Dr. Frances explains, "The organizational principle that brought cohesion to *DSM-III* and *DSM-IIIR* was the omnipresent leadership of Bob Spitzer, who chaired every work group, nursed every detail, and wrote every word."[204]

What Spitzer did to radically alter the idea of mental illness was to suggest two new diagnostic criteria, which allegedly distinguish normal human behavior from abnormal or sick. First of all, Spitzer declared that if symptoms (behavior, mindsets, and emotions) did not impair normal function or cause distress, then the person in question did not actually have a disease. So for example, a child could have all the criteria necessary to meet a diagnosis of ADHD, yet if the child is benefiting from his symptoms or the behaviors are not impairing his life, then according to Spitzer's theory, the child is not sick.[205] Throughout

---

[202] For more on Spitzer's influence, see Robert Whitaker, *Anatomy of an Epidemic: Magic Bullets, Psychiatric Drugs, and the Astonishing Rise of Mental Illness in America* (New York: Broadway Books, 2010), 268-72.

[203] Bentall, *Madness Explained*, 53-58.

[204] Frances, *Saving Normal*, 172.

[205] Renowned secular authors on ADHD Hallowell and Ratey insist that "for many people, ADD is not a disorder but a trait, a way of being in the world." In their view, ADHD is a "positive character quality" that provides many gifts and talents until behavior becomes maladaptive (Edward M. Hallowell and John J. Ratey, *Delivered from Distraction: Getting the Most out of Life with Attention Deficit Disorder* [New York: Ballantine Books, 2005], 4).

the *DSM-5* this subjective qualification is referred to as "clinically significant disturbance/impairment,"[206] and the former APA president, Jeffery Lieberman, refers to it as "subjective distress."[207] Lieberman is correct: distress is a subjective opinion that considers human impairment—especially for a lengthy time—to be an abnormality within evolutionary ideology.

Second, Spitzer also added the qualifying element of time or duration: the person being evaluated must have the symptoms for x amount of time. Typically, this duration amounts to a period of six months across various life settings. Not only did these two moves add to Kraepelinian theory and redefine the secular paradigm, but they also reveal just how subjective the current secular construct truly is. A specific timeframe (such as six months) is an objective qualification, but a timeframe itself is subjective. Spitzer and his *DSM* committee could have subjectively chosen one, two, or twenty years for the prequalifying duration of mental illnesses. They also have not explained why a timeframe is objectively needed at all. Spitzer's subjective time qualifications seemingly provided a much-needed demarcation line between normal and abnormal, but they did not add any scientific or objective value to Kraepelin's original theory or objectively establish a standard of normalcy.

With these two new qualifications of mental illness in place (subjective distress and duration), suddenly, if a person was anxious beyond six months, then he or she was sick with anxiety disorder rather than being a normal person struggling with anxiety. If an individual was sad and hopeless to the point that it impaired his or her life for longer than six months, then he or she

---

[206] APA, *DSM-5*, 20.

[207] Lieberman, *Shrinks*, 136.

was to be diagnosed as "clinically depressed." Anxiety and sadness/hopelessness are certainly not insignificant, but claiming them as physical disease based on subjective criteria alone does not make anxiety or sadness medical issues.

Likewise, Spitzer's clinical distress/impairment makes mental illness a matter of a patient's and doctor's perceptions or beliefs. Equipped with this new distress qualification, clinicians could view any mindsets, behaviors, emotions, and desires that impair life as a disease rather than a normal human experience or even a character flaw. Such a reality also explains why almost any negative human emotion, behavior, desire, or mindset can be found in the ever-growing list of over 400 mental illnesses found in the *DSM*.[208] Lieberman notes of Spitzer's redesign of the secular construct of mental illness:

> This was a definition of mental illness radically different from anything before. Not only was it far removed from the psychoanalytic view that a patient's mental illness could be hidden from the patient herself, but it also amended Emil Kraepelin's definition, which made no reference to *subjective distress* and considered *short-lived conditions* to be illnesses too [emphasis added].[209]

This new widely-accepted, yet subjective, definition of mental illness led British psychiatrists Richard Hunter and Ida Macalpine to state,

> There is not even an objective method of describing or communicating clinical findings without subjective interpretation and no exact and uniform terminology which conveys precisely the same to all. In consequence there is wide divergence of diagnosis, even of diagnoses, a steady flow of new terms and an ever-changing nomenclature, as well as a surfeit of hypotheses which tend to be presented as fact. Furthermore, etiology remains speculative, pathogenesis largely obscure, classifications predominantly symptomatic and hence arbitrary and possibly ephemeral; physical

---

[208] Reznek, *Peddling Mental Disorder*, 89.

[209] Lieberman, *Shrinks*, 136.

treatments are empirical and subject to fashion and psychotherapies still only in their infancy and doctrinaire.[210]

The *DSM* and its proposed construct of mental illnesses, then, are not actually scientific discoveries or validated definitions of disease; rather they are man's—at times, only one man's—subjective hypotheses about human nature and human experiences.

Although it is important to understand what Spitzer did to redefine mental illness, it is also helpful to understand why his alteration to Kraepelin's original construct was necessary for psychiatry in general and the ongoing acceptance of the current construct. At the same time the APA was revising the *DSM-II*, the LGBT movement was pressuring the APA to drop homosexuality as a disease in the impending release of the *DSM-III*. Spitzer was caught in a dilemma. A refusal to comply with LGBT demands would have been politically disastrous: psychiatry itself would be marginalized as homophobic and irrelevant. If, however, he and his task force did remove homosexuality from the *DSM-III*, then what had been for years dogmatically held and advertised as a brain-disorder and/or a genetic defect (homosexuality) would no longer be considered an illness without any explanation other than political pressure.[211] Furthermore, if homosexuality were removed entirely, then it would expose the APA to be a sham and their so-called diseases as subjective social and political opinions.[212] Either way, the APA seemed set to lose credibility and authority.

---

[210] Richard Hunter and Ida Macalpine, quoted by Mark Micale and Roy Porter, *Discovering the History of Psychiatry* (New York: Oxford University Press, 1994), 10.

[211] Bentall, *Madness Explained*, 57.

[212] Lieberman, *Shrinks*, 126.

This dilemma was solved by Spitzer's inventing the concept of clinically significant impairment and changing the label of "Homosexuality Disorder" to "Sexual Disorder not Otherwise Specified."[213] Those who were living a homosexual lifestyle but felt it impaired their life or caused them distress could still fall under the label of being disordered, and those who were content with their lifestyle could live their lives as they wished without being considered mentally ill. Dr. Lieberman explains the environment in which Spitzer was forced to rewrite the construct of mental illness:

> Spitzer found himself in a troubling intellectual bind. On one hand, the antipsychiatry movement was stridently arguing that all mental illnesses were artificial social constructions perpetuated by power-hungry psychiatrists. Like everyone at the APA, Spitzer knew these arguments were taking a toll on the reliability of his profession. He believed that mental illnesses were genuine medical disorders rather than social constructs—but now he was about to declare homosexuality to be exactly such a social construct. If he disavowed homosexuality, he could open the door to the antipsychiatrists to argue that other disorders, such as schizophrenia and depression, should also be disavowed. Even more worrying, perhaps insurance companies would use the decision to rescind the diagnosis of homosexuality as a pretext to stop paying for any psychiatric treatments.[214]

Spitzer's created qualifiers (clinical impairment and duration) would form the basis of the new Kraepelinian construct still sustained today, but they were instituted as a way to redefine illness in order to remain relevant and maintain authority. Spitzer's neo-Kraepelinian criteria and redefining of illness exist, not because they are scientifically or medicinally sound, but because without these criteria, the general construct of mental illness and its individual disorders would both have been discarded for what they truly are—unscientific and subjective opinions.

---

[213] Kutchins and Kirk, *Making Us Crazy*, 91.

[214] Lieberman, *Shrinks*, 125.

This understanding of mental illness as a subjective construct and the product of faith may very well be what led one of the most renowned psychiatrists in American history Jerome Frank to state that "psychotherapy may be the only treatment that creates the illness it treats."[215] In a similar manner, Szasz states, "Whereas in modern medicine new diseases were discovered, in modern psychiatry they were invented. Paresis was proved to be a disease; hysteria was declared to be one."[216] Even alleged experts and advocates of secular theories admit that what they have created and marketed to be illness differs greatly from physical illness. Francis Mondimore, professor of psychiatry and behavioral sciences at Johns Hopkins and considered by many to be an authority on bipolar disorder, says,

> When we think about illnesses of the body, we usually think of diseases that have a beginning, a middle, and an end. Take, for example, pneumonia, and infection of the lungs caused by bacteria. The disease begins when fever, cough, chest pains, and breathing problems appear. These symptoms build and worsen over a period of hours or sometimes days. . . . Bipolar disorder is very different from these diseases, because it does not simply have a beginning, a middle, and an end.[217]

The way that the *DSM* and psychiatry seemingly escape this fact is by creating a new definition of illness, imposing materialism onto that which is spiritual or immaterial and applying Spitzer's qualifiers to normal but impairing mindsets, emotions, and behavior. With the publishing of the *DSM-III* in the early 1960s psychiatry began to convince many that the mind was organic and non-spiritual, simply a part of the brain. This leap of faith enabled secularists to assign sickness to the non-material part of the patient (they claim as material) in the same way valid

---

[215] Hubble, Duncan and Miller, *Heart and Soul of Change*, 2.

[216] Szasz, *Myth of Mental Illness*, 12.

[217] Mondimore, *Bipolar Disorder*, 32-33.

physical illnesses were categorized and diagnosed. Dr. Greenberg comments,

> Spitzer did something else to juice the credibility of the *DSM-III*, something that no one else had done, at least not in a diagnostic manual: he tried to define disease. . . . Spitzer understood from the beginning that the commonsense definition of disease — "a progressive physical disorder with known pathophysiology" — simply couldn't be stretched to cover mental illness. He finessed this problem by proposing that disease was only one of a number of medical disorders — conditions that had "negative consequences . . . an inferred or identified organismic dysfunction, and an implicit call to action." Mental disorder, he argued, was a "medical disorder whose manifestations are primarily signs or symptoms of a psychological (behavioral) nature." This was a clever move on Spitzer's part, acknowledging that mental illnesses were not diseases in the usual sense, even as he preserved their place in "real medicine."[218]

Seemingly overnight, the world was impacted by the redefining of spiritual and mental struggles as a new type of disease — mental illness:

> The appearance of the *DSM-III* was thus an event of capital importance not just for America but for the world psychiatry, a turning of the page on psychodynamics, a redirection of the discipline toward a scientific course, a reembrace of the positivistic principles [materialism] of the nineteenth century, a denial of the antipsychiatric doctrine of the myth of psychiatric illness.[219]

Szasz also explains how such a new definition of illness became widely accepted without any validating evidence:

> With the decline of religion and the growth of science in the eighteenth century, the cure of (sinful) souls, which had been an integral part of the Christian religions, was recast as the cure of (sick) minds, and became an integral part of medical science.[220]

Christians and secularists both agree that people struggle with impairing behaviors, mindsets, and emotions, but their opposing

---

[218] Greenberg, *Book of Woe*, 114-15.

[219] Shorter, *History of Psychiatry*, 302.

[220] Szasz, *Myth of Psychotherapy*, preface xxiv.

worldviews yield dramatically different explanations, definitions, and remedies for these problems.

Their Shared Worldview

The evolutionary construct of mental illness is an all-or-nothing anthropology because its materialistic view of humanity excludes all other approaches to mental problems and interpretations of impairing behaviors.[221] In the general sense, there are two mutually exclusive approaches to understanding and defining human nature, and one must embrace one or the other through faith. The secular psychiatrist Peter Breggin touches on the necessity to place one's faith in one of the two anthropological views and subsequent theories of mental health:

> If people who express seemingly irrational ideas are best understood mechanistically, then these people are broken, disordered, or defective devices. If we take the viewpoint that they are persons, beings, or souls in struggle, then an infinite variety of more subtle possibilities comes to mind for understanding and helping those who seem mad, crazy, or deranged.[222]

Our anthropological views will determine what we believe about mental health, how to approach the subject and the individual, and how to remedy the immaterial faculties. If a therapist views a patient through the lens of Darwinian Theory and materialism, then he or she will also approach spiritual and behavioral problems mechanistically. If, however, the patient is seen as created in the image of God, then any problems will make sense only in light of God's wisdom, and the therapist can approach the patient empathetically as a fellow struggling soul. So the discussion on mental illness is clearly founded on a proper discussion of faith, authority, and anthropology.

---

[221] Steve and Hilary Rose, *Alas, Poor Darwin: Arguments against Evolutionary Psychology* (London: Vintage Publishing, 2001), 1-3.

[222] Peter Breggin, *Toxic Psychiatry*, 25.

Ultimately, for the Christian, it must also be founded on right theology.

The disconcerting reality is that the secular theory concerning both anthropology and mental illness is based entirely upon an unbiblical worldview that worships the creature over the Creator. Kraepelin and Freud believed that the story of creation and Adam's fall were myths, and so they devised theories accordingly.[223] Likewise, both men were determinists. Szasz notes of Freud,

> Here, then, lie the crucial similarities between Marxism and Freudianism: each is a historicist doctrine attributing all-pervasive causal influences on conduct to a single type of "cause" or human circumstance.... Freud assigned the same powers to family-historical, or so-called genetic-psychological circumstances. Both of these unsupported—and, as [Karl] Popper shows, unsupportable and palpably false—doctrines have nevertheless become widely accepted in our day. The sanction of legal recognition has, of course, long supported the psychiatric view that certain kinds of "abnormal" behaviors were "caused" by antecedently acting "mental diseases." This view was simply extended to behaviors of all kinds by Freud and his supporters, and has been embraced even by many of his opponents, especially the behaviorists.[224]

Such humanistic, materialistic, and, deterministic philosophies and subsequent practices (as with sociobiology and genomic theories) are "conceptual legacies of Darwinism."[225] The ideas of Kraepelin, Freud, Spitzer and current key figures in secular psychiatry are firmly rooted in the theory of evolution. The application of this theory to the problems of the mind has produced the modern, almost universally accepted construct of mental illness.[226]

---

[223] Szasz, *Psychiatry*, 40.

[224] Szasz, *Myth of Psychotherapy*, 6.

[225] Satel and Lilienfeld, *Brainwashed*, 153.

[226] Cherry, "What is Humanistic Psychology?"

The shared worldview of Kraepelin, Freud, and Spitzer also explains why the APA chooses to leave the definition of normalcy ambiguous. The APA's true undisclosed standard of normalcy suggests that people are mentally strong, morally sound, and self-reliant (only the strong survive). When someone, then, is impaired, in distress, or does not morally or socially measure up over a period of time, this deviation from the evolutionary ideal or theorized standard of normalcy constitutes an abnormality, what psychiatrists call mental illness. Though the secular authorities on mental illness wish to keep the definition of normalcy imprecise and unwritten, evolutionary theory asserts that all humans are mentally and intellectually strong or that they are progressing toward an idea of perfection or a superhuman race. Thus, according to an evolutionary worldview, any deviation from a theoretical mental, emotional, or behavioral perfection can be perceived as mental illness. The ideology of the secular worldview leaves everyone falling short of its theorized concept of humanity.

CHAPTER 4 – DIAGNOSING MENTAL ILLNESS

If the *DSM* is not scientifically based and not the truly objective and reliable bible of psychiatry that some claim, then the diagnostic process for most mental illnesses based upon the *DSM* also lacks validity, reliability, and objectivity. Dr. Allen Frances states,

> The absence of biological tests is a huge disadvantage for psychiatry. It means that all of our diagnoses are now based on subjective judgments that are inherently fallible and prey to capricious change. It is like having to diagnose pneumonia without having any tests for the viruses or bacteria that cause the various types of lung infection.[227]

In his book on bipolar disorder, Dr. Mondimore also conveys this reality:

> At least once a month, it seems, I see a patient who asks to be "tested for bipolar disorder." It's not an unreasonable request. Unfortunately, it's not a request that can be satisfied — not yet. There's no blood test or x-ray or biopsy that can diagnose bipolar disorder (and, for that matter, there is none that can be used to confirm the diagnosis of most of the problems psychiatrist treat).[228]

Though advocates of mental illnesses (such as ADHD, schizophrenia, bipolar disorder, and anxiety disorders) claim that these constructs have been scientifically proved and genetically caused, no scientific data or tests are available to actually make such claims.[229] Faith, and not science or medicine, undergirds such claims. In the medical textbook, *Mental and Neurological Public Health: A Global Perspective*, the authors assert

---

[227] Frances, *Saving Normal*, 12.

[228] Mondimore, *Bipolar Disorder*, 29.

[229] Ibid.

that "whereas strong medical epidemiology was based on mapping and correlation cases and causes, the cause of mental illness was strictly unknown (and still is for the major functional groups)."[230] Dr. Peter Breggin also remarks concerning the secular construct of bipolar disorder:

> There are no known biological causes of depression in the lives of patients who routinely see psychiatrists. There is no known genetic link in depression. There is no sound drug treatment for depression. The same is true for mania: no biology, no genetics, and little or no rational basis for endangering the brain with drugs.[231]

The diagnostic process for non-neurological disorders found in the *DSM* is completely subjective and based upon the established authority's subjective opinion rather than any valid medical reason. In fact, Dr. Panksepp in his *Textbook of Biological Psychiatry* reveals that one of psychiatry's major goals must be to decide which disorders objectively exist and how they know those disorders exist, instead of merely insisting they are real because behaviors can be observed and categorized:

> A major goal is now to seek deeper levels of understanding, which confronts us with a series of interlocking dilemmas. Epistemologically, we must resolve what major disorders objectively exist, and we must be able to specify how we know they exist, above and beyond mere surface symptoms.[232]

Symptoms of mental illness (specifically chosen behavior) are not only the grounds for diagnoses, they are also products of one's belief system. Ethan Watters explains, "Symptoms of mental illness are the lightning in the zeitgeist, the product of culture and belief in specific times and specific places."[233] Yet

---

[230] Patel et al., *Mental and Neurological Public Health*, 477.

[231] Breggin, *Toxic Psychiatry*, 183.

[232] Panksepp, *Biological Psychiatry*, 18.

[233] Watters, *Crazy Like Us*, 3.

symptoms are the scientific basis of the diagnosis; they are observable and what patients most easily recognize.[234] In fact, psychiatrists are not diagnosing in the medical and scientific sense they claim. Instead, their alleged medical-practices amount to describing and labeling people according to their symptoms in order to fit them into their non-medical and non-scientific system. Neuropsychiatrist Sydney Walker notes,

> Causative understanding — knowing why symptoms occur — is the foundation of medical care. Doctors are trained to begin with a patient's symptoms, and work from there — by taking compulsively thorough medical and personal histories, conducting in-depth physical and neurological examinations, ordering appropriate neurophysiologic evaluations and biochemical studies, and evaluating the results of brain scans and other tests, until a definitive diagnosis can be made. This medical detective work, known as the *deductive differential diagnoses*, is the cornerstone of medicine. But modern psychiatry has attempted to shortcut the process with a book known as the *Diagnostic and Statistical Manual*. In doing so, psychiatry has replaced the science of diagnosis with the pseudoscience of labeling.[235]

The claim that diagnosing mental illness is a scientific endeavor is far from the truth: the diagnoses are often little more than a categorization of people according to their self-reported or others-testified similar behaviors. Walker further remarks:

> Such patients eventually learn the hard way that a label is not a diagnosis. Saying someone is "depressed" or "anxious" is a far cry from finding out what causes the depression or anxiety; it's comparable to a pediatrician saying a child has "spots" without bothering to find out whether the spots are caused by measles, poison ivy, or staphylococcus. Patients who have been "diagnosed" as having manic depression, anxiety disorder, attention deficit hyperactivity disorder, and so on, haven't been diagnosed; they've merely been described. Such labels, are simply a sophisticated-sounding way of making quick and superficial observations.[236]

---

[234] Emil Kraepelin, *Lectures on Clinical Psychiatry* (New York: Hafner, 1968). See also Greenberg, *The Book of Woe*, 38.

[235] Sydney Walker, *A Dose of Sanity: Mind, Medicine, and Misdiagnosis* (New York: John Wiley and Sons, 1996), 5.

[236] Ibid., 5.

Patients and their families may initially be relieved by receiving a label that describes their behaviors, feeling as though they now know what is wrong. Labeling from a trustworthy figure—even if incorrect—can provide temporary hope that the problem has been identified and that something can be done to treat the patient's problems. There can also be a sense of comfort in the naming and categorizing of behavior that makes the patient feel that he or she is not alone.

However, many times the psychiatric label becomes part of the patient's identity and results in behavior that conforms to the expected label. Further if patients and family members discover that the psychiatrist merely labeled the problem, not actually knowing what was wrong or identifying a biological disease, then hope is often dashed.

The secular paradigm simply does not offer an objective way to differentiate causes of an individual's behavior, mindsets, and emotions. Doctors must determine without any scientific tests, system of measurements, or biological markers if symptoms are caused by genuine brain-malfunction, circumstances, personal choice, or acting. In fact, Dr. Frances comments on the true nature of what secularists claim in the *DSM* to be disorders:

> Some mental disorders describe short-term states, others life-long personality; some reflect inner misery, others bad behavior; some represent problems rarely or never seen in normals [sic], others are just slight accentuations of the everyday; some reflect too little self-control, others too much; some are intrinsic to the person, others are culturally determined some begin early in infancy, others emerge only late in life; some affect thought, others emotions, behaviors, interpersonal relations some seem more biological, others more psychological or social.[237]

Likewise, if a doctor insists that an individual has a mental illness, then, within the secular paradigm, he or she does —

---

[237] Frances, *Saving Normal*, 17.

unless another doctor claims the initial diagnosis was a misdiagnosis. Dr. Szasz notes,

> Because there are no objective methods for detecting the presence or establishing the absence of mental diseases, and because psychiatric diagnoses are stigmatizing labels with the potential for causing far-reaching personal injury to the stigmatized person, the "mental patient's" inability to prove his "psychiatric innocence" makes psychiatry one of the greatest dangers to liberty and responsibility in the modern world.[238]

If the established authority subjectively perceives or simply prefers to deem someone's actions to fit a label, he or she has the power to label that person or not.

One of the most profound examples of the overwhelmingly subjective nature of the secular paradigm of mental illness can be observed in the research and writings of David Rosenhan, professor of law and psychology at Stanford University. In 1973, in the celebrated journal *Science*, he published an article that undermined the current secular construct by exposing the subjective nature of both the *DSM* and its diagnostic process. This article "On Being Sane in Insane Places"[239] was not a philosophical paper but rather a report on an experiment that he had conducted in psychiatric hospitals.

Unbeknownst to the various mental wards, Rosenhan had successfully placed numerous "healthy" individuals (his students) varying in race and age into twelve different hospitals across multiple states without any of them ever being recognized to be fake patients. To be admitted, they simply had to state that they were hearing voices. The experiment was overwhelming: the pseudo-patients were time and time again diagnosed as schizophrenic and admitted to each of the hospitals. Not only

---

[238] Szasz, *Psychiatry*, 3.

[239] David Rosenhan, "On Being Sane in Insane Places," *Science* 179, no. 4070 (January 19, 1973): 250-58.

did normal people convince the so-called experts that they were sick by simply their rhetoric, but even after stating they were in fact normal and not sick, many were still held in the hospitals and their confession of normalcy still diagnosed as schizophrenia. Of course the psychiatric establishment was furious with Rosenhan's study and his publication exposing the subjectivity of the mental illness construct. Dr. Frances comments on the result of Rosenhan's study: "Psychiatrists looked like unreliable and antiquated quacks, unfit to join in the research revolution just then about to modernize the rest of medicine."[240]

But Rosenhan did not stop there. He challenged one hospital to willingly participate in his next study, which they gullibly accepted. His challenge was simple:

> Over the coming year, I will send in another round of imposters to your hospital. You try to detect them, knowing full well that they will be coming, and at the end of the year we see how many you catch.[241]

Over the course of the next year, the hospital staff worked hard to identify all potential fake patients. Out of 193 new patients who entered the hospital, the psychiatrists identified 41 as potential impersonators. But Rosenhan had once again pulled the rug out from under them and had further exposed the subjectivity and unreliability of the diagnostic process. He accomplished this goal by not sending a single pseudo-patient to the hospital as he had stated would happen. His study, along with many others who have conducted similar experiments with similar results, clearly shows that distinguishing between fake and real or misdiagnosis and valid diagnosis is well-nigh

---

[240] Frances, *Saving Normal*, 62.

[241] To read Rosenhan's full report, see http://www.bonkersinstitute.org/rosenhan.html.

impossible.[242] The inability for science to know the true cause of moral behavior along with the belief that only science can yield valid answers to mental problems permits the current construct to exist.

Today, pseudo-patients still exist, but no one is sending them to hospitals; they are willfully entering themselves. Who is a fake patient or normal and who is abnormal is left to the subjective opinions of the evaluator and the patient. Again, this is not to insinuate that behaviors, mindsets, and emotions are not real or that people are not burdened with genuine mental struggles. But the way in which these true problems are perceived, explained, and approached are in question. While the struggles are real, understanding whether the struggles are normal or abnormal behavior is completely subjective in the current construct of mental illness.

Furthermore, within the field of mental health, it is common for one doctor to label an individual as mentally ill while another doctor claims the label is a misdiagnosis. Lieberman's explanation of his experience with a patient whom he believed

---

[242] In 1 Samuel 21:12-15, King David pretended to be a mad man by drooling and repeatedly marking the door of the gate. His behavior was judged by Achish the king of Gath to be crazy (14). For David, it was fear that led him to behave as madman. It is difficult to know what is truly taking place in someone's heart and why a person behaves in a certain way without discerning those behaviors through God's wisdom because only God can see the spiritual heart of man. In David's case, his behavior was a direct result of his fear, as revealed in the text. It is also worth noting that in antiquity, valid neurological defects (such as autism), all types of brain damage, and demon possession were all categorized as madness. David's pretending to be "mad" does not mean that he was acting demon possessed or that he was acting in a way that we would call mentally ill. By the description of his behaviors, he could have been pretending to have a valid neurological injury such as an anoxic injury. Dr. Kyziridis explains, "At one point, all people who were considered 'abnormal', whether due to mental illness, retardation, or physical deformities, were largely treated the same" (Theocharis C. Kyziridis, "Notes on the History of Schizophrenia," *German Journal of Psychiatry* 8 [2005]: 42–48).

had been misdiagnosed by another doctor reveals the confusion and imprecision in the current system:

> I now felt confident about my diagnosis that her pathology was due to developmental injury and substance-induced toxicity. Her prior diagnoses of schizophrenia [from another doctor], schizoaffective disorder, and bipolar disorder had been reasonable guesses since in reality she suffered from a "phenocopy" of mental illness, meaning that she was exhibiting symptoms that mimicked a DSM-defined illness without suffering from the actual illness.[243]

If the symptoms fully qualify an individual to have a mental illness yet the patient is diagnosed as having a phenocopy or symptoms that simply "mimic an alleged illness," how does one know objectively what is wrong with the patient? What if all human disorder has explainable causes apart from the psychiatric system? The answers, again, are that clinicians cannot know objectively and reliably what is true. What is ironic, however, is that the *DSM* contains a mental illness called "malingering" (lying).[244] Maybe Lieberman's diagnosis is likewise incorrect and the young lady is actually stricken with the secular disease of "pretending to be sick when you aren't."[245] Szasz comments,

> Psychiatrists have asserted that malingering, too, is a form of mental illness. This presents us with the logical absurdity of a disease which, even when it is deliberately counterfeited, is still a disease.[246]

Maybe the patient actually should have been diagnosed with "other specified" schizophrenia and bipolar since she did not meet the criteria but still seemed to fit the categories. All of these

---

[243] Lieberman, *Shrinks*, 238.

[244] APA, *DSM-5*, 726-27.

[245] "Malingering," https://www.psychologytoday.com/conditions/malingering.

[246] Szasz, *Myth of Mental Illness*, 13.

possibilities could be right, and all of them could be wrong within the secular construct; it all depends upon the opinion of the evaluator. In truth, "guessing" — as Lieberman rightly suggests — is what commonly takes place in the diagnostic process and in the secular paradigm.

Another illustration that reveals the subjective nature of the secular construct is the overwhelming number of individuals who obtain a diagnosis of ADHD in order to obtain Ritalin. Since the diagnosis of ADHD is based on normal behaviors, a patient needs merely to tell the doctor that he or she meets the criteria. This practice is widespread:

> Pharmaceutical abuse is on the rise among teens, surpassing the combined rates of crack/cocaine, Ecstasy, heroin and methamphetamine abuse, according to the Partnership for a Drug-Free America. Experts predict the trend will continue because the pills are inexpensive and widely available. "Unlike cocaine, you can get Ritalin very cheaply from your friends because all they need is their co-pay," Teitelbaum said. "There's a great availability." *Some students will go to great lengths to trick physicians into writing prescriptions for Ritalin.* "There is no question that the modern student is smart, and smart enough to go to a doctor and to tell them exactly what the *symptoms are of attention deficit disorder, to get stimulants* [emphasis added]."[247]

People don't try to dupe doctors by claiming that they have cancer in order to get chemotherapy, and no doctor worth his salt would simply believe a patient's unfounded claims. When it comes to valid physical disease, physicians verify.

In contrast, psychiatrists and physicians have no choice but to believe a person's testimony when attempting to diagnose the mind, unless of course a clinician judges one's thoughts and behaviors to be delusions, hallucinations, or malingering. Then the patient's testimony is denied as true. This subjectivity establishes and maintains the system that psychiatrists and

---

[247] "Risky Ritalin Abuse during College Exam Week," http://ihealthbulletin.com/archive/2007/05/14/risky-ritalin-abuse-during-college-exam-week/.

many other professionals endorse, so they must abide by its demands and constraints.

Additionally, clinicians are not typically observing behavior, but rather they listen to the testimony of the patient and people in the patient's sphere of influence. But people think and behave differently in various life environments (e.g., clinical tests and office visits versus real life).[248] Psychiatrist David Allen remarks,

> People do not act the same way in all social contexts. . . . We have different "faces" or masks which we apply to ourselves in different environments. Not infrequently, these masks are meant to manipulate others to get them to do what we want them to do. Some of the masks are so rigid and pervasive that they become what therapists call a "false self." . . . Additionally, I never cease to be amazed at how mental health professionals and researchers seem to believe that they really know what is going on in a patient's or a research subject's life based solely on the self report of the patient, or solely on the reports of the patient's intimates, or even on the reports of people like teachers who observe the behavior of children in only one context that includes thirty other distracting students. If these professionals were asked if they believe that people often act differently in public than they do behind closed doors, they would of course say yes, but they seem to develop amnesia for this fact in discussions and in studies.[249]

The diagnostic system represented by the *DSM* fits people into psychiatric categories instead of identifying and healing their true problems.

Changing Beliefs

Furthermore, what the *DSM* dogmatically claims as a mental illness can be reconsidered if the presiding authority's beliefs change or if the APA is politically or socially pressured enough to do so. In some cases this change is not merely a case of altering or revamping aspects of a diagnosis but renouncing a

---

[248] Hubble, Duncan, and Miller, *The Heart and Soul of Change: What Works in Therapy*, 303.

[249] David Allen, "Why Psychotherapy Efficacy Studies Are Nearly Impossible,"https://www.psychologytoday.com/blog/matter-personality/201212/why-psychotherapy-efficacy-studies-are-nearly-impossible.

dogmatically claimed illness. One striking example of such a change is psychiatry's about-face in regards to so-called homosexuality disorder.

> No one knows what causes heterosexuality, homosexuality, or bisexuality. Homosexuality was once thought to be the result of troubled family dynamics or faulty psychological development. *Those assumptions are now understood to have been based on misinformation and prejudice* [emphasis added]. Currently there is a renewed interest in searching for biological etiologies for homosexuality. However, to date there are no replicated scientific studies supporting any specific biological etiology for homosexuality. Similarly, no specific psychosocial or family dynamic cause for homosexuality has been identified, including histories of childhood sexual abuse. Sexual abuse does not appear to be more prevalent in children who grow up to identify as gay, lesbian, or bisexual, than in children who identify as heterosexual.[250]

The APA claims that they can no longer endorse the belief that homosexuality is a mental disorder, since no scientific evidence exists. Yet it once held a different position (which it admits as prejudice) even when no scientific evidence existed. So while this change is marketed and appears to be scientifically based, it is in reality a change in their belief system, since no scientific evidence exists to prove either position. To say it differently, secular science is more faith in theory than objective fact. As beliefs change, so too does the so-called science. Two former reviewers for the *DSM-III*, Drs. Herb Kutchins and Stuart Kirk explain:

> The homosexuality controversy illustrates [a major] theme, namely, that science is often not central to the decision to include or exclude a diagnosis from [the] *DSM*. The dispute over the inclusion of homosexuality in the *DSM* was not about research findings. *It was a 20-year debate about beliefs and values.* Although the professionals who formulated diagnoses couched their arguments in the language of science, the actual influence of empirical data was negligible. *More often than not, the issues were settled by political compromises that promoted personal interests* [emphasis added].[251]

---

[250] http://www.psychiatry.org/lgbt-sexual-orientation.

[251] Kutchins and Kirk, *Making Us Crazy*, 56.

Likewise, according to the textbook *Biological Psychiatry*,

> The extent to which diagnostic schemes are influenced by societal standards is highlighted by the disappearance of homosexuality as a psychiatric disorder in the more recent versions of the manual. . . . It also partly reflects the emergence of new human rights movements. Scientific advances and cultural tensions will continue to permeate diagnostic practices since some "disorders" are only extremes of normal human temperamental variability (especially among the Axis II disorders), while others, to put it metaphorically, are more likely to reflect "broken parts" in the brain (most abundantly in the severe Axis I disorders).[252]

Though psychiatry suggests that science is the authority behind the ideas of mental illness, the facts reveal that fallible, subjective humans are the true established authority on what is normal human temperament. Psychiatrist Lawrie Reznek explains the same reality concerning feminist lobby groups winning out over psychiatrists' proposed Masochistic Personality Disorder (MPD)[253] proposed by chair of the *DSM-III* task force, Allen Frances:

> Although the categories introduced were defined in terms of observable features, this left open the possibility that the categories were included because of political motivations rather than because of any scientific discoveries. The debate over the inclusion of MPD illustrates the political nature of psychiatric diagnosis. In fact, *DSM-III* made it easier to include psychiatric diagnoses that were political in nature which masqueraded as science. By defining groups targeted for political oppression by empirical criteria, *DSM-III* obscured the political purpose of the classification, sanitizing it with the illusion of science.[254]

Dr. Greenberg also remarks of the alleged homosexuality disorder,

> When doctors said homosexuality was a disease, that was not an opinion, let alone bigotry-it was a fact. When they wrote that fact down in the *DSM*, it was not a denunciation. It was a diagnosis. . . .

---

[252] Panksepp, *Biological Psychiatry*, 18.

[253] Masochistic Personality Disorder is associated with female submissiveness, and many believe it encourages domestic violence.

[254] Reznek, *Peddling*, 91-92.

> The prejudices and fallacies behind psychiatric diagnoses, and even the interest they serve, are as invisible to all of us, doctors and patients alike, as they were to . . . all those doctors who "treated" homosexuals.[255]

The creators of the secular construct are willing to dogmatically claim an illness as valid until social pressure and popular opinion force them to change their position. Science and medicine, though claimed as fundamental to the secular construct, are not the true foundation for the construct of mental illness.

Likewise, Spitzer's introduction of "subjective distress" allowed secular authorities to deny that they were wrong and still appease the gay and lesbian activists. Instead of removing homosexuality outright, which would openly reveal the subjective unreliable nature of the diagnostic system, Spitzer left the disorder in the new *DSM-III* and imposed his idea of subjective distress. Lieberman notes,

> Spitzer began to argue that if there was no clear evidence that a patient's condition caused him emotional distress or impaired his ability to function, and if a patient insisted he was well, then a label of illness should not be imposed. If someone claimed that she was content, comfortable, and functioning adequately, then who was the psychiatrist to say otherwise? . . . By endorsing the principle of subjective distress, Spitzer made it plain that homosexuality was not a mental disorder and on its own did not warrant any kind of psychiatric intervention.[256]

If mindsets, emotions, and behaviors are detrimental and have duration, then within the secular construct, they must be perceived to be an illness. However, if the patient does not perceive his mindsets, emotions, or behavior as distressing, then the patient should not be considered to be mentally ill. The adjusted psychiatric disorder of homosexuality not only brought about this new definition and approach to mental and

---

[255] Greenberg, *Book of Woe*, 5-7.

[256] Lieberman, *Shrinks*, 126.

behavioral struggles, but it also revealed the diagnostic process and the construct of mental illness to be a subjective belief system: any unwanted or impairing mindset, emotion, or behavior that lasts a significant amount of time can be considered a mental illness.

Individual Experts

Not only are the American Psychiatric Association (APA), the American Psychological Association, the National Institute of Mental Health (NIMH), the National Alliance for the Mentally Ill (NAMI), the World Health Organization (WHO),[257] and the *DSM*[258] (to name a few) all established as authorities in the mental health field, but within the secular paradigm, individuals are also set up as authorities on specific disorders. For example, Dr. Frederick Goodwin, former head of the NIMH, is considered by most mental health professionals to be "the world's leading authority on bipolar disorder."[259] For every individual disorder proposed in the *DSM*, there is at least one authority on the subject. But what if these alleged authorities are established by pharmaceutical companies and then paid well by these same companies to research and/or market their agendas? Dr. Whitfield comments,

---

[257] "Will the *DSM* be superseded by the *ICD*? There is little justification for maintaining the *DSM* as a separate diagnostic system from the *ICD* in the long run, particularly given the U.S. government's substantial engagement with *WHO* in the area of classification systems. But, said Reed, 'there would still be a role for the *DSM*, because it contains a lot of additional information that will never be part of the *ICD*. In the future, it may be viewed as an important textbook of psychiatric diagnosis rather than as the diagnostic Bible'" (American Psychology Association, "ICD vs. DSM," 63).

[258] The American Psychiatric Association owns the full rights of the *DSM* and currently controls the system.

[259] "In the Spotlight: Dr. Frederick Goodwin," http://www.healthcentral.com/bipolar/frederick-goodwin.html.

> It has [corrupted the integrity of research and scientific literature] by paying or otherwise manipulating researchers and authors to speak in favor of their drugs.... Unfortunately for the consumer, the drug industry does not always act in their best interest. In addition, drug companies pay *experts* [emphasis added] to promote their drugs. For example, Dr. Robert Spitzer who headed the 1980 *DSM* committee that recommended GAD as a disorder was also paid by drug companies to research drug treatments for anxiety disorders.[260]

Similarly, head of the *DSM-IV*, Dr. Allen Frances, comments on physicians whom he calls the "highfliers":

> They write the most prescriptions for multiple medications per patient at the highest average doses, and every patient may be on the same drug cocktail. They also probably charge the most per visit but may have trouble remembering the patient's name or problem. They attend drug company events religiously and may sometimes speak at them, extolling the latest new wonder drug. Their office is a magnet for drug salespeople, all of whom are on a chummy first-name basis with the secretary. The office is strewn with drug company presents and paraphernalia. Our highflier probably drives the best car and lives in the best house.[261]

Within the secular construct of mental illness, expert and national speaker often translate into well-paid friend of pharmacology.

Controlled Opinions

Not only is the *DSM* considered by psychiatrists and therapists to be the authority on defining and diagnosing mental illness, but only those who are approved and granted authority can properly diagnose from the *DSM*. Essentially, the APA has made their institution to be the ultimate authority. The *DSM* establishes this element of control when it states, "Clinical training and experience are needed to use *DSM* for determining a diagnosis."[262] Dr. Mondimore writes,

---

[260] Whitfield, *Truth about Mental Illness*, 220, 223.

[261] Frances, *Saving Normal*, 216-17.

[262] APA, *DSM-5*, 5.

> Because the *DSM* contains a list of psychiatric diagnoses followed by succinct and clearly written "criteria" for making those diagnoses, it also has the unfortunate effect of making psychiatric diagnosis look deceptively easy. It is tempting for individuals who have no psychiatric training to use this series of symptoms checklists to diagnose mental illness. Well, why not? First of all, it is only with an enormous amount of training and experience *that one can gain an appreciation for the very wide range of normal emotions and behaviors and have a sense of what falls outside this normal range* [emphasis added]. Significant clinical experience and judgment are needed to decide what constitutes an "expansive mood" or an "increase in energy" that is clinically significant.[263]

Dr. Mondimore's faulty logic suggests that only those who are thoroughly trained can recognize abnormalities that are based on the non-existent psychiatric standard of normalcy. Similarly, psychiatrist Joseph Pierre suggests that

> The good news for mental health consumers is that clinicians worth their mettle don't rely on the *DSM* as a bible in the way that many imagine, checking off symptoms like a computer might and trying to 'shrink' people into the confines of a diagnostic label. A good psychiatrist draws upon clinical experience to gain empathic understanding of each patient's story, and then offers a tailored range of interventions to ease the suffering, *whether it represents a disorder or is part of normal life* [emphasis added].[264]

The *DSM* currently allows the secular paradigm to exist, but the clinicians and therapists reveal themselves to be the true authority by subjectively deciding who is mentally ill and thus who is normal. However, Mondimore also writes that even trained clinicians may not be qualified to make proper diagnoses.[265] In other words, only those who are considered authorities—those who agree with and are immersed in the established secular paradigm—can make proper diagnoses and decide what behavior is normal/abnormal. This suggestion is precisely what psychiatrists are taught in school—to be

---

[263] Mondimore, *Bipolar Disorder*, 56.

[264] Pierre, "A Mad World."

[265] Mondimore, *Bipolar Disorder*, 56.

authoritative.[266] But research shows that efficacy in diagnosing and counseling is not a matter of "mastery, education, or experience," but rather the "performance of the therapist" that enables faith and hope, which can bring about change.[267]

With or without possessing authority, therapists and physicians must use the *DSM* according to their construct to determine alleged illnesses based on symptoms. Yet such a diagnosis is subjective in nature. Greenberg comments,

> They have yet to figure out just exactly what mental illness is, or how to decide if a particular kind of suffering qualifies. The *DSM* instructs users to determine not only that a patient has the symptoms listed in the book (or, as psychiatrists like to put it, that they meet the criteria), but that the symptoms are "clinically significant." But the book doesn't define that term, and most psychiatrists have decided to stop fighting about it in favor of an I-know-it-when-I-see-it definition (or saying that the mere fact that someone makes an appointment is evidence of clinical significance).[268]

In essence, Greenberg reveals that if someone goes to get help from a therapist or psychiatrist, then they are declaring themselves to have "clinically significant impairment" in the opinion of many professionals. To further complicate the diagnostic process, for most "mental illnesses" listed in the *DSM*,

---

[266] Breggin, *Toxic Psychiatry*, 379.

[267] "Consider the sizable body of research that shows that the personal qualities of individual therapists contribute as much as three times more to the variance of psychotherapy outcome than the model or theoretical orientation that is used. Even adherence to a carefully designed manual or treatment protocol has failed to prevent widely varying outcomes among therapists! These results, in combination with others showing a weak correlation between amount of training and clinical outcome, strongly suggest that admission to training and eventually credentialing be based on the ability to perform rather than the mastery of various theories or techniques. The survival of the mental health professions, in other words, will be better ensured by identifying empirically validated treaters [sic] rather than empirically validated treatments" (Hubble, Duncan, and Miller, *Heart and Soul of Change*, 439). This point will be developed further in volume 5 of this series under the discussion of psychotherapy.

[268] Greenberg, *Book of Woe*, 14.

clinicians have the option to diagnose people with a mental illness if they feel like the client has a disorder without meeting the *DSM* criteria. Typically, in the *DSM-IV*, this option is listed under "Not Otherwise Specified"[269] or in the *DSM-5* as "Other Specified" and "Unspecified."[270] Dr. Mondimore notes this reality concerning alleged bipolar disorder,

> If you look at the end of the section on bipolar disorder in the fifth edition of the *DSM* of the American Psychiatric Association, you will see the category "bipolar disorder not elsewhere classified" (also, simply, "bipolar NEC"). This odd category exists because the developers of the *DSM* recognized that there are patients who *seem to have some kind of bipolar disorder* [emphasis added] but who don't meet the diagnostic criteria for bipolar I or II or cyclothymia.[271]

However secularists might attempt to justify these indefinable catch-all categories in their classification system, their existence completely undermines the supposedly objective-scientific nature of the *DSM* as a tool for establishing criteria (mostly behaviors) for actual diseases. The true basis for diagnoses is not medical in nature, but the clinician's subjective opinion. It appears, then, that the *DSM* is simply a medical/scientific prop that allows the APA to control society through their subjective system of categorization and labeling.

---

[269] For the diagnosis of ADHD as one example, see *DSM-IV*, 93.

[270] For the diagnosis of ADHD as one example, see *DSM-5*, 65-66.

[271] Mondimore, *Bipolar Disorder*, 44.

CHAPTER 5 – CONTROLLING MENTAL ILLNESS

We have seen that the secular paradigm has established human wisdom as both the author and authority behind today's current secular theories of mental illness, but we must still address two more prominent groups who greatly influence theories, so-called discoveries, and treatments of all mental illnesses: the pharmaceutical industry and the Federal Drug Administration (FDA).

The involvement/control of large pharmaceutical companies working with policymakers and the FDA is significant in the mental health field—so too is the deception they spread.[272] Dr. Allen Frances remarks,

> The legal psychiatric drug industry has thrived through the aggressive spread of misinformation. Big Pharma has almost unlimited financial resources, political punch, marking prowess, and greed in the pursuit of new markets and bigger profits. But all this could be reversed on a dime if politicians had the motivation to do so. None of the following policy changes would be hard to enforce. Most them are already in place in the rest of the world and work well to better contain, if not entirely eliminate the excessive use of prescription drugs.[273]

Their influence and control is often facilitated by their spread of "misinformation," which is directly tied to psychiatry.[274] One example is found in the companies' relationships with clinicians,

---

[272] For more on how the pharmaceutical companies and corrupt politics have created a crisis in the mental health construct, see Lawrie Reznek, *Peddling Mental Disorder*, 89.

[273] Frances, *Saving Normal*, 212.

[274] For more on the pharmaceutical companies' influence and the corruption prevalent within the secular construct, see Lawrie Reznek, *Peddling Mental Disorder*.

authors, and speakers who have been groomed to become authorities on various mental illnesses. For example, Dr. Fred Goodwin, a specialist on bipolar disorder, often receives great sums of money from pharmaceutical companies in return for his advocacy and marketing capabilities.[275] This association has caused many to question his statements in support of psychotropic drugs when the scientific studies contradict his statements.[276] Or take as another example, "internationally recognized authority on ADHD,"[277] author, and speaker Russell Barkley who also "receives or has received research support, acted as a consultant and/or served on a speaker's bureau for Eli Lilly and Company, Shire Pharmaceuticals Group plc, and McNeil Pediatrics."[278] Allen Schwarz reports about Barkley:

> Dr. Barkley, who has said that "S.C.T. is a newly recognized disorder," also has financial ties to Eli Lilly; he received $118,000 from 2009 to 2012 for consulting and speaking engagements, according to propublica.org. While detailing sluggish cognitive tempo in the Journal of Psychiatric Practice, Dr. Barkley stated that Strattera's performance on sluggish cognitive tempo symptoms was "an exciting finding." Dr. Barkley has also published a symptom checklist for mental health professionals to identify adults with the condition; the forms are available for $131.75 apiece from Guilford Press, which funds some of his research. Dr. Barkley, who edits sluggish cognitive tempo's Wikipedia page, declined a request to discuss his financial interests in the condition's acceptance.[279]

---

[275] John M. Grohol, "Dr. Fred Goodwin Update," http://psychcentral.com/blog/archives/2008/12/04/dr-fred-goodwin-update/.

[276] Ibid.

[277] "Russell A. Barkley, Ph.D.," http://www.russellbarkley.org/.

[278] "Conflicts of Interest for Practice Parameters Not Listed in Parameter," http://www.aacap.org/AACAP/Resources_for_Primary_Care/Practice_Parameters_and_Resource_Centers/Conflicts_of_Interest_for_Practice_Parameters_Not_Listed_in_Parameter.aspx.

[279] Schwarz, "Idea of New Attention Disorder."

Conflicts of interest are common practice within the current system. But is such a system ethical? Is it possible that such conflicts of interest might be responsible for the widespread acceptance of unproven theories of mental illness? Should not the product of such a conflicted body of contributors be skeptically examined rather than heedlessly accepted? Dr. Frances recognizes these concerns:

> A legitimate question has been raised about the motivations of the people working on *DSM-IV*—did we go soft on diagnostic inflation because of a financial conflict of interest? The concern arises from recent study showing that 56 percent of our experts had some financial connection to drug companies. The assertion has been made that the companies were pulling strings behind the scenes, directly or subtly, to bend decisions toward more diagnosis and more treatment. The question is certainly legitimate because we had no formal conflict of interest policy or vetting system. This omission was a silly mistake on our part—the necessity simply never occurred to any of us when we began working the fairly innocent pre-Prozac days of 1987.[280]

Dr. Charles Whitfield also acknowledges,

> During this time, countless articles and books were published to support [psychiatry's] growing idea that most mental illness is due to a genetically transmitted brain problem. With the help of the drug industry, this theory spread throughout medicine and the helping professions and eventually into the *public belief system* [emphasis added].[281]

The commonly accepted belief system, though unproven, enables the APA's ongoing authority and control.

Like the *DSM* contributors, the American Academy of Child and Adolescent Psychiatry has a long list of clinicians and advocates of secular constructs who are directly tied to

---

[280] Frances, *Saving Normal*, 75.

[281] Charles Whitfield, *Truth about Mental Illness, The Truth about Mental Illness: Choices for Healing* (Deerfield Beach, FL: Health Communications, 2004), preface xvi.

pharmaceutical companies.[282] This collaboration has become such a problem that in 2011 the federal government had to stop the new ADHD guidelines due to the undisclosed connections of these companies with psychiatrists. Such unethical connections cross over into the political realm and include the well-known Joseph Biederman:

> Dr. Joseph Biederman, is currently under U.S. Congressional investigation for his undisclosed financial ties to the pharmaceutical industry. Dr.Biederman, whose studies are cited more than 70 times in the draft ADHD guidelines, has confessed to receiving up to US$1.6 million to research and promote specific drugs, clearly a conflict of interest.[283]

A definite—yet not always disclosed—conflict of interest exists between many prominent psychiatrists/physicians, politicians, and the drug companies. These relationships greatly impact the funded research, the findings, and the current theories of mental illness that they promote.[284] Dr. Whitfield explains,

> The politics of psychiatry, psychology, and other special interest groups and government are intertwined and complex, and they often spin off to harm the health consumer as much as they may help.[285]

Unfortunately, in many cases, the FDA is not protecting consumers from such corruption, but instead, the FDA is adding

---

[282] "Conflicts of Interest for Practice Parameters Not Listed in Parameter," American Academy of Child and Adolescent Psychiatry, http://www.aacap.org/AACAP/Resources_for_Primary_Care/Practice_Parameters_and_Resource_Centers/Conflicts_of_Interest_for_Practice_Parameters_Not_Listed_in_Parameter.aspx.

[283] "New Federal ADHD Guidelines Halted due to Undisclosed Drug Company Connections of US Psychiatrist," http://www.cchr.org.au/media-releases/189-new-federal-adhd-guidelines-halted-due-to-undisclosed-drug-company-connections-of-us-psychiatrist.

[284] Allen Schwarz, "Still in a Crib."

[285] Whitfield, *Truth about Mental Illness*, 38.

to the corruption. In an article published on the website of *Psychology Today*, Ray Williams asserts,

> Drug companies also have an impact on governments and social policy. The industry seeks direct influence at a government level by employing political lobbyists and contributing large sums of money to political parties and campaigns. In the United States, there are more pharmaceutical industry lobbyists than Congress members. The lobby budget for 1999 and 2000, at $197 million dollars, was $50 million dollars larger than the drug industry's nearest rivals, the insurance and telecommunications industries. On top of this, the industry makes generous contributions to election campaigns.[286]

Likewise, the documentary *American Addict* exposes

> The blatant corruption of the whole FDA, pharmaceutical companies and insurance company trinity of terror. Corporatism is alive and well in America, and the pharm. industry and its cozy relationship with the federal government is a specific microcosm of this power structure.[287]

Dr. Whitefield also acknowledges this unethical relationship:

> Due to the fact that government agencies such as the FDA and its equivalents in other countries are commonly enmeshed with the drug companies and the academics that research and write about mental illness and its treatment, they are increasingly unable to objectively monitor and when necessary restrict the drug companies or restrain them to protect the public.[288]

The well-documented examples of such corruption are abundant and overwhelming. Both the U.S. government and large pharmaceutical companies are major players in the hierarchy of authority when it comes to mental illness.

But let us return to the issue of faith. Since these connections exist, how can a person trust these authorities to offer valid research and reveal empirical findings? Charles Seife touches on

---

[286] Ray Williams, "How the Drug Companies Are Controlling Our Lives," http://www.psychologytoday.com/blog/wired-success/201105/how-the-drug-companies-are-controlling-our-lives-part-1.

[287] *American Addict*, directed by Sasha Knezev and Gregory Smith (Torrance, CA: Pain MD Productions, 2013).

[288] Whitfield, *Truth about Mental Illness*, 220.

the lack of trustworthiness when he comments on how drug money is undermining scientific objectivity:

> The problem is not just with the drug companies and the researchers, but with the whole system—the granting institutions, the research labs, the journals, the professional societies, and so forth. No one is providing the checks and balances necessary to avoid conflicts. Instead, organizations seem to shift responsibility from one to the other, leaving gaps in enforcement that researchers and drug companies navigate with ease, and then shroud their deliberations in secrecy.[289]

His solution to this corruption is more transparency and the dissolving of any unethical relationships that can invalidate studies, "that way the scientific community decides whether a study is ethical and when the experiment is done, how far to *trust* [emphasis added] the results."[290] Trust/faith is essential to approaching mental illness and even essential to interpreting allegedly scientific data. Research professor in the department of physiology and biophysics at Georgetown University Medical Center, Dr. Candace Pert says, "Science at its most exalted is a truth-seeking endeavor, which encompasses the values of cooperation and communication, based on trust—trust in ourselves and in one another."[291] Even within the scientific community, faith is a foundational presupposition to science and medicine, yet those who shape psychiatric policy and practice are not making a strong case to be trusted. Thus those who accept the positions of the pharmaceutical industry and the FDA must face the fact that embracing these views is a choice to believe the foundational doctrine of evolutionary psychology

---

[289] Charles Seife, "How Drug Company Money Is Undermining Science," *Scientific American* 307, no. 6 (December 1, 2012), 56.

[290] Ibid.

[291] Candace B. Pert, *Molecules of Emotion: The Science behind Mind-Body Medicine* (New York: Scribner, 1997), 315.

and to ignore the overwhelming subjectivity, human error, false claims, political corruption, invalidated theories, and even outright fraud involved in the creation of those positions. Believing in the secular construct, whether knowingly or through default is to establish a secular body as the authority and Darwinian theory as the foundational underlying anthropology.

CHAPTER 6 – UNDERSTANDING MENTAL ILLNESS

The secular idea of mental illness is an unproven and unreliable construct, which attempts to explain unwanted or detrimental human behaviors, mindsets, and emotions within the framework of Darwinian thinking. While the construct is a man-made theory or ideology, it exists as an attempt to explain or understand a reality. Unlike a construct, the reality (which the construct attempts to explain) can stand alone independent of the created theory and can often be explained by other constructs (whether valid or not). Psychiatrist Allen Frances explains,

> The labeling of mental disorder has evolved over time because the lens of cultural attention extracts figure from ground in many different ways. We see elephants in clouds if we look for them. But could equally well find whales or rabbits if these better fit our preconceptions—the cloud doesn't have to change for people to see different shapes in it. Psychiatric diagnosis is seeing something that exists, but with a pattern shaped by what we expect to see.[292]

So, the construct is not verified fact but a theory which seeks to explain "something that exists" or resolve a problem through the lens of one's worldview. While at times constructs can be helpful, they must be formed with several necessary components in order to be helpful, reliable, objective, sustained, and even potentially validated.

Logically, the first integrant to a sustainable construct is a clear, tangible reality that permits the construct to exist. In the case of the construct of mental illness, there are several key realities: (1) mental impairments and struggles commonly exist,

---

[292] Frances, *Saving Normal*, 36.

(2) the mind is different from the brain, and (3) common human nature creates patterns of human behavior.

The second necessary piece to a reasonable and reliable construct is the terms or criteria that constitute the paradigm and attempt to explain or approach reality. Prominent psychiatrists—primarily Emil Kraepelin and Bob Spitzer—have created the current neo-Kraepelinian system of categorization (the philosophy and terms or criteria) which enables the construct of mental illness and the individual disorders now contained in the *DSM*. However, the problem with the terms utilized in the secular paradigm is that they are not fixed or objective. As we observed with the changes to the *DSM-III* under Bob Spitzer with the elimination of the construct of homosexuality, secular terms both in the construct of mental illness and in sub-constructs (individual disorders) are ever changing with the addition of new labels and sub-constructs and the revision or disregard of terms within individual disorders. In fact, the "other specified" and "not specified" criteria of the individual constructs are terms that eliminate all other proposed integrants and expose the subjective opinion of the evaluator to be the true construct. Dr. Frances describes the chaos created by such loose standards of policy and diagnosis:

> When clinicians follow the criteria, they achieve reasonable agreement. Without them, there is poor agreement. Each clinician becomes a law unto himself, and the result is a confusing Babel of clashing, idiosyncratic voices. . . . The final decision where to set the bar is always a judgment call; the research never renders a clear and compelling answer forcing the choice of one particular threshold in preference to other possibilities.[293]

In this way the current construct forces individual doctors to create their own subjective "law." This subjectivity casts a

---

[293] Frances, *Saving Normal*, 24.

shadow of unreliability over the entire construct.[294] The *DSM* is so unreliable, that in their review of the *DSM-III*, Drs. Herb Kutchins and Stuart Kirk assert that "the *DSM* revolution in reliability has been a revolution in rhetoric, not in reality."[295] Dr. Bob Spitzer in an interview with the *New Yorker* also remarks,

> To say that we've solved the reliability problem is just not true. . . . It's been improved. But if you're in a situation with a general clinician it's certainly not very good. There's still a real problem, and it's not clear how to solve the problem.[296]

Dr. Frances agrees:

> To my way of thinking, the reliability of the *DSM*—although improved—has been oversold by some people. . . . From a cultural standpoint, reliability was a way of authenticating the *DSM* as a radical innovation. . . . In a vacuum, to create criteria that were based on accepted wisdom, as a first stab was fine, as long as you didn't take it too seriously.[297]

The problem with reliability brings us to the final necessary integrant for a valid and reliable construct: the terms of the paradigm must be consistently and objectively upheld. This required coherence must be both internally established and externally enforced. In other words, if one or more of the terms are contradictory, self-defeating, or subjective, then the construct is not reliable, true, and may not be even logical. Likewise, if those who are to enforce a construct change or disregard the established and accepted terms according to their individual thinking, then the construct loses its value to explain the reality

---

[294] Bentall, *Madness Explained*, 43.

[295] Kutchins and Kirk, *Making Us Crazy*, 50.

[296] Bob Spitzer quoted by Alix Spiegel, "The Dictionary of Disorder: How One Man Revolutionized Psychiatry," *New Yorker* (January 3, 2005), http://www.newyorker.com/magazine/2005/01/03/the-dictionary-of-disorder.

[297] Ibid.

for which it exists. In truth, those who alter a construct (even slightly), which they have allegedly accepted as valid, create a new construct on which to rest their faith.

Yet, this practice of constant revision and inconsistent adherence is precisely what occurs repeatedly within the construct of mental illness. Even a cursory review of books on specific mental illnesses and the general paradigm of mental illness reveals that each author has formed his or her own individual construct that varies, sometimes slightly and other times drastically, from the *DSM* or the established psychiatric authority. Such variation also explains why a specific construct or disorder may be regarded as overdiagnosed by some clinicians and underdiagnosed by others. These arguments are never made in reference to valid physical diseases and reliable diagnoses such as cancer or diabetes, but they are expected discussions surrounding subjective constructs.

The secular construct of mental illness has established terms and insisted that society accept this system. The original construct still utilized today is Emil Kraepelin's, but with each revision of the *DSM*, with each new established authority in the APA, and with each newly created illness, a new version of Kraepelinian orthodoxy is born. While the major tenets of Kraepelin's original theory are intact, the neo-orthodoxy of psychiatry has added new terms and ever-changing criteria in attempt to validate or refine Kraepelin's construct. Dr. Richard Bentall explains,

> In Kraepelin's original system, there were only two or three major categories of psychosis. However, in order to make the *DSM* exhaustive, its authors have dramatically increased the number of definitions included in successive editions of the manual, and have also included catch-all 'not otherwise specified' diagnoses in order to sweep up anyone who does not fit the criteria for a specific disorder. At the same time, in order to ensure that diagnoses are mutually exclusive, the authors have had to include special exclusion rules to

limit the possibility that patients will fall into more than one category.[298]

However, these alterations have not only attempted to redefine illness, they have also exposed the subjective and unreliable nature of the *DSM*, the subjective and unreliable nature of the secular construct, and the invalid position of authority that psychiatry claims to rightfully own. Still, the *DSM-5* insists that

> While *DSM* has been the cornerstone of substantial progress in reliability, it has been well recognized by both the American Psychiatric Association (APA) and the broad scientific community working on mental disorders that past science was not mature enough to yield fully validated diagnoses—that is, to provide consistent, strong, and objective scientific validators of individual *DSM* disorders. The science of mental disorders continues to evolve.[299]

By their own admission, their constructs of mental illness are not yet valid. In spite of the fact that psychiatry admits that the sub-constructs are ever changing and not yet validated, the *DSM* insists that speculation should not exist in valid science/medicine but that speculation is necessary in its construct. It even goes as far as to say that its place of authority depends upon the careful future changes to its construct:

> The *DSM-5* Task Force overseeing the new edition recognized that research advances will require careful, iterative changes if *DSM* is to maintain its place as the touchstone classification of mental disorders. Finding the right balance is critical. *Speculative results do not belong in an official nosology*, but at the same time, *DSM* must evolve in the context of other clinical research initiatives in the field [emphasis added].[300]

Simply put, believing the secular construct today positions individuals in a place of error tomorrow since prominent

---

[298] Bentall, *Madness Explained*, 69.

[299] APA, *DSM-5*, 5.

[300] Ibid. Nosology is a branch of medicine dedicated to the task of classifying disease.

professionals admit their construct is ever-changing, unreliable, speculative, and completely subjective. Lest a person think this point is overstated, the former chair of the *DSM-IV* task force remarks: "What seem now to be fanciful myths were once the best science of the time, and our current best science will itself in the not-too-distant future be seen as no more than fanciful myth."[301] Such an honest admission by one of the key authors of the current construct of mental illness should cause readers to seriously question if the current major scientific claims are worthy of their faith. For secularists, however, there seems to be no repercussion for claiming their theory as scientific dogma today and fanciful myth tomorrow. These same theorists will form new theories and insist that these alleged scientific discoveries be accepted without question. They skillfully claim that their science is evolving, when in truth, they simply change their opinions.

Constructs are easy to form but especially when it comes to mental illnesses. Since mental illnesses are based on the current popular and agreed-upon psychiatric opinion without any biological means to validate or invalidate such claims, new disorders can be created out of any unwanted and enduring behavior. Dr. Reznek explains,

> The ease of constructing new mental disorders goes a long way to explaining the proliferation of mental disorders that we have already described. Because there is no way that validity can act as a break on the construction of these categories, they get multiplied beyond necessity. From just five mental disorders described in 1880, we now have around four hundred, an 8,000 percent increase. With more and more mental disorders available to succumb to, this in part explains why the prevalence of mental disorders has climbed form 1-2 percent of the population one hundred years ago to around 50 percent of the North American population today.[302]

---

[301] Frances, *Saving Normal*, 36.

[302] Reznek, *Peddling Mental Disorder*, 89.

The ease of constructing new psychiatric illnesses enables an ever-expanding list and number of people who can fit into the construct.

Constructs are not only easy to form, but they can also be formed around almost any reality. Dr. Bentall illustrates this fact in discussing how the construct or taxonomy of astrology has been formed around the existence of stars:

> Consider the real-life example of astrology, a system of classification that provides a fool's-gold standard against which to evaluate modern psychiatric diagnoses. Like diagnoses, star signs are supposed to describe human characteristics and to predict what will happen to people in the future. Although there is no evidence to support these claims, astrology is a system of classification that continues to capture the imagination of large numbers of otherwise intelligent people. Indeed, a recent poll revealed that almost one quarter of American adults believe in astrological theories.[303]

Dr. Bentall later explains that reliability and validity are both needed for a theory to be proved and accepted as objective truth.

> We saw that one way of assessing the usefulness of a diagnostic system is to measure its reliability. However, the example of astrology illustrates the limitation of this approach. Star signs are highly reliable (we can all agree about who is born under Taurus), so reliability alone cannot ensure that a diagnostic system is scientific. Further tests of the validity of the system are necessary to determine whether it fulfills the functions for which it has been designed. We can test the validity of astrological theories by seeing whether people born under the sign of Libra really are well-balanced, or whether most Scorpios really do meet the beautiful stranger of their dreams in the first quarter of the year. Similarly, we can evaluate the validity of diagnostic categories by seeing whether they lead us to useful scientific insights or helpful clinical predictions. Of course, although reliability does not guarantee validity, it is obvious that a diagnostic system cannot be valid without first being reliable. *Unless psychiatrists and psychologists can agree about which patients suffer from which disorders there is no possibility that the process of diagnosis will fulfill any useful function.* ... For the most part, modern psychiatric diagnoses fail to meet adequate standards of reliability. Some readers might therefore be forgiven for wondering whether there is any point in proceeding to examine validity evidence in detail. However, there are two good reasons for doing so. First, some readers, particularly those who have trained in the mental health professions, may require further persuasion before abandoning long-held assumptions about the nature of madness. Second, as we study the validity of psychiatric diagnoses we will encounter evidence that

---

[303] Bentall, *Madness Explained*, 67.

will be useful when attempting to construct a scientific alternative to the Kraepelinian system.[304]

Constructs or classification systems are easily created within the secular mental health field. If we take the three necessary integrants of a construct presented above and apply them to a common human activity, we can see how easy it is to form a construct and convince people of its importance and validity. For example, lying is a real and impairing problem in modern American society. The reality of the problem validates it as a foundation for a psychiatric construct. From here we must develop terms or conditions similar to those found in the *DSM*; these definitions are the second component of an acceptable construct. For these criteria we could suggest that if a child (minimum age of four) lies in one or more settings in his life more than five times in a period of six months and these lies cause significant impairment to him or those around him, then he should be labeled as having "Truth Deficit Disorder." Once we have agreed upon our criteria and those under our authority have accepted these new terms and label of TDD, we must not only ensure that when lying occurs it is viewed through the criteria of the construct, but that the terms of the paradigm are upheld. Proper marketing and continued research allows the construct to grow in acceptance and to eventually sway most of society to only view lying through the lens of the construct and as a brain disease rather than a moral character issue.

Some people attempt to deny the reality that mental illness is a construct which intends to influence people to view aspects of life and human nature through an evolutionary worldview.

---

[304] Ibid.

Others, however, admit that the construct of mental illness is simply one way to explain anthropology.[305]

Mental illness as suggested by the APA and its *DSM* is a social construct. We recall the words of the influential and once-prominent Dr. Allen Francis: "We saw *DSM-IV* as a guidebook, not a bible—a collection of temporarily useful diagnostic constructs, not a catalog of 'real' diseases."[306] With every *DSM* revision, come new labels and corresponding constructs, attempting to convert normal detrimental or unwanted human behavior into theorized abnormal brain-dysfunction. This construct of mental illness and its contained sub-constructs, however, are poorly constructed, unreliable, unenforced, unsustainable, and lack validity.

---

[305] Frances, *Saving Normal*, 21.

[306] Ibid., 73.

CHAPTER 7 – SEEKING CAUSES OF MENTAL ILLNESS

At the center of the secular paradigm of mental health exists an often heated yet necessary debate on what causes alleged mental illness. Such philosophical debates center not on specific etiologies (causes) of disorders per se, but on whether mental illness as a whole is caused by nature, by nurture, or by both. Dr. Charles Whitfield comments on this debate:

> Throughout history we have looked for the cause of mental illness, and we still don't know it. The two major theories have long been and remain: nature (genes, biology) versus nurture (environment, family). Our mistake has been to focus on only one or the other. In fact, based on our current knowledge, it appears that both nature and nurture are active factors in most people with mental disorders.[307]

Similarly, behavioral neuroscientist and psychologist Jaak Panksepp writes,

> It is surely not off the mark to claim that the single most important scientific question for biological psychiatry is the accurate decoding of the basic neural nature of affective values [nature] and related cognitive experiences. . . . The cognitive, behavioral, and affective sciences must devote equal effort to understanding the embeddedness of mind in brain, body, environment, and culture [nurture]; otherwise essential components will be overlooked. Only by blending these perspectives judiciously, without inflaming simple-minded polarities such as nurture versus nature, is psychiatric practice well served.[308]

Still others believe such discussions are damaging. One editor of the *American Psychiatric Publishing Textbook of Forensic Psychiatry* asserts,

---

[307] Whitfield, *Truth about Mental Illness*, preface xv.

[308] Panksepp, *Biological Psychiatry*, 4.

> I will not attempt to resolve the historical and sociological debates that have characterized the history of psychiatry. As some historians have acknowledged, the once-fashionable distinction between the external (nurture) and internal (nature) histories of medicine and science is not productive. The development of psychiatry cannot be understood entirely as an internal process related to scientific advancement. It also cannot be fully understood by interpretations that evaluate only external social forces such as the desire for professional aggrandizement or, more recently, the impact of managed health care on medical practice.[309]

Though this series of books will discuss both nature and nurture and conclude from Scripture that they are both relevant to the believer's mindsets, emotions, and behaviors, the insightful believer will recognize that the human nature is more than genetics and biology as Dr. Whitfield's statement suggests. The nature of mankind is in fact both physical and spiritual; he is psychosomatic.

In order to form a truly biblical construct of mental illness, then, one must consider true human nature as well as how all aspects of life affect and shape who people are. Such conclusions, by necessity, will require faith and will include a remedy that addresses both human nature and life (nurture). No matter which philosophical approach to mental illness one ultimately chooses, faith is the vital beginning and sustains his position.

---

[309] Robert Simon and Liza Gold, eds., *American Psychiatric Publishing Textbook of Forensic Psychiatry* (Washington, DC: American Psychiatric Publishing, 2010), 5.

CHAPTER 8 – ACCEPTING THE BIBLICAL WORLDVIEW

Like all secularists, Christians must approach the issues of human nature, authority, and the mind-brain connection with faith. Unlike the secular construct, however, Scripture insists that faith is required to discern or interpret the observable, repeatable, and measureable realities of the world (what secularists call science) and accept views of God and man.[310] Additionally, the Bible is not searching for answers about humanity's immaterial nature; it claims to already possess them.

The Bible Claims the Importance of Faith

The Bible claims that faith is foundational to establishing authority and approaching and defining human nature. Though such faith claims are often rejected out of hand, it is an inescapable fact that all scientific theory, whether valid or pseudo-science, is founded on presuppositional belief. Renowned American scientist and philosopher Karl Popper once said of the approaches to science,

> For the critical attitude is not so much opposed to the dogmatic attitude as super-imposed upon it: criticism must be directed against existing and influential beliefs in need of critical revision – in other words, dogmatic beliefs. A critical attitude needs for its raw material, as it were theories or beliefs which are held more or less dogmatically. Thus science must begin with myths, and with the criticism of myths.[311]

---

[310] This book uses the secular term "science" to describe the observable, repeatable, and measureable realities in the world so as to not cause confusion.

[311] Karl Popper, *Philosophy of Science: An Historical Anthology*, ed. Timothy McGrew, Marc Alsperctor-Kelly, and Fritz Allhoff (New York: Wiley and Sons, 2009), 480.

Both valid science and pseudo-science begin with foundational faith. Whether or not people believe that the secular paradigm of mental illnesses is science or pseudo-science, faith is the real foundational issue.

For the believer, faith in the sufficiency of God and his Word to meet our needs of life and godliness must come before any science that those who reject God might present as fact. While we certainly should never reject valid truth or ignore alleged discoveries, we must above all choose to either establish the Creator, not the creation, as the highest authority. If alleged science precedes our faith, then we not only reject God and His Word as our supreme authority, but we also invite the deceptive and destructive philosophies and traditions of human wisdom and forego biblical discernment.

In the case of mental illness, the religion of scientism based on the theory of evolution is the accepted authority and object of faith, and the construct of mental illness is one byproduct. In Colossians 2:8, Paul warns of this very type of thing:

> Therefore, as you received Christ Jesus the Lord, so walk in him, rooted and built up in him and established in the faith, just as you were taught, abounding in thanksgiving. See to it that no one takes you captive by philosophy and empty deceit, according to human tradition, according to the elemental spirits of the world, and not according to Christ.

In regards to a construct of mental illness, we all have faith in either God's authority or human authority. Though valid science is relevant and can provide visible standards and illuminate truth, it is only a small part of God's overall design to reveal His character, explain human existence and nature, and offer the only remedy for mental anguish. This view of science (as a construct to describe the visible revelation and creation of God) as subservient to inspired truth found in the Bible obviously conflicts with the modern exaltation of secular science as the primary tool for acquiring knowledge and understanding people.[312]

Though the Christian faith and practices and the secular beliefs and approaches to science are clearly antithetical, many believers still place their faith in secularists' purported science over the unchanging and proven Word of God to describe behaviors, mindsets, and emotions. Shmuel Boteach, prominent American rabbi, warns, however, that

> Too often in the past, "scientific" positions (which are contrary to Judaism) have been adopted without delving into the validity of those scientific assertions: this is bad for the truth if the theories are wrong, and the situation is worsened [from] . . . belief in the false or inaccurate scientific dogma. Another, perhaps more important, reason to intensify the debate on this issue in particular is the way in which Darwinism can sometimes be manipulated to promote dangerous morals and ethics.[313]

What secular thinking sometimes claims to be science is really an application of Darwinian Theory.

Just as secular science accepts human wisdom by faith, so the Christian embraces God and His wisdom by faith (Heb 11:6). The biblical view, however, insists that faith is the starting point for discovering science. Hebrews 11:1 says, "Now faith is the assurance of things hoped for, the conviction of things not seen." Secularists do not use the word *faith* to characterize their alleged scientific activities and conclusions, yet faith and the more scientific term *hypothesis* are not too different when carefully compared. In fact, Karl Popper asserts,

> Hume was right in stressing that our theories cannot be validly inferred from what we can know to be true—neither from observations nor from anything else. He concluded from this that our belief in them was irrational. If "belief" means here our inability to doubt our natural laws, and the constancy of natural regularities, then Hume is again right: this kind of dogmatic belief has, one might

---

[312] Szasz, *Psychiatry*, 56.

[313] Shmuel Boteach, *Moses of Oxford: A Jewish Vision of a University and Its Life* (London: Andre Deutsch Ltd, 1995), 484.

> say, a physiological rather than a rational basis. If, however, the term "belief" is taken to cover our critical acceptance of scientific theories—a tentative acceptance combined with an eagerness to revise the theory if we succeed in designing a test which it cannot pass—then Hume was wrong. In such an acceptance of theories there is nothing irrational. There is not even anything irrational in relying for practical purposes on well-tested theories, for no more rational course of action is open to us.[314]

According to Popper, faith is rational and is a prerequisite to any applied science. What God has not explained in natural revelation or science, He has either explained in supernatural revelation in His Word or it is not necessary for people to know. In humanistic and Darwinian thinking, however, it is the responsibility of humanity to explain its entire existence and that of the natural world. Popper comments,

> Assume that we have deliberately made it our task to live in this unknown world of ours; to take advantage of the opportunities we can find in it; and to explain it, if possible (we need not assume that it is), and as far as possible, with the help of laws and explanatory theories. If we have made this our task, then there is no more rational procedure than the method of trial and error—of conjecture and refutation: of boldly proposing theories; of trying our best to show that they are erroneous; and of accepting them tentatively if our critical efforts are unsuccessful.[315]

But God's Word has already explained that which cannot be seen or understood through the scientific process concerning the mind, emotions, desires, and behaviors. When it comes to the soul or mind, people do not need to look beyond what God has revealed in His Word to understand true human nature. Instead, our responsibility is simply to trust God and His wisdom on issues which He has clearly explained and which have never been disproved. The only reason people attempt to explain a person's unobservable nature differently than God does is that they have rejected God's Word as their ultimate authority.

---

[314] Popper, *Philosophy of Science*, 481.

[315] Ibid.

While scientism attempts to explain the unobservable mind, it is simply a system of faith that has been somewhat successful in making that which is spiritual or non-physical seem scientific and medical. Both Darwinian and Kraepelinian theories should be understood as belief systems or constructs rather than as scientific fact or even scientific in nature. Still, secularists conveniently choose Darwinian ideology. Popper later remarks,

> The method of trial and error is not, of course, simply identical with the scientific or critical approach — with the method of conjecture and refutation. The method of trial and error is applied not only by Einstein but in a more dogmatic fashion, by the amoeba also. The difference lies not so much in the trials as in a critical and constructive attitude towards errors; *errors which the scientist consciously and cautiously tries to uncover in order to refute his theories with searching arguments, including appeals to the most severe experimental tests which these theories and his ingenuity permit him to design* [emphasis added].[316]

True scientists do not dogmatically claim an unproven theory as true. They establish a theory based on faith and attempt to prove it as true or recognize the theory as false. When their theories are proved wrong, however, they admit discovered errors in their theories, and thus they dismiss such theories as invalid.[317]

Though faith is essential to our discussion, God's wisdom does not reject or ignore valid science. Instead, it demands that natural and supernatural revelation be connected:

> For by it [faith] the people of old received their commendation. By faith we understand that the universe was created by the word of God [faith in creation vs. evolution], so that what is seen was not made out of things that are visible.[318]

Faith is the prerequisite for understanding the physical world, but science is not essential for faith; in other words, though

---

[316] Popper, *Philosophy of Science*, 481.

[317] The issue of science will be developed further in volume 3 of this series.

[318] Hebrews 11:2-3.

science (what is observable, repeatable, and measureable) can be beneficial to our faith, it is not necessary for faith. This truth in Hebrews allows us to understand why secular authorities on most mental disorders deny faith in God as Creator and instead believe in the so-called science of evolution.[319] The reality is that man's presuppositional faith determines his definition of and approaches to science.

As Scripture lays out the pattern of human existence, we see that faith is a requirement to discern scientific claims. Whether one believes in the brain-disease model of mental health,[320] that the world is flat, that groups of people are genetically defective, that draining blood from a patient provides mental health,[321] or that Pluto is a planet, the necessity of faith to understand and accept science can be seen throughout history.

To declare that something is scientifically validated, however, does not mean that it is. In spite of clear evidence, society in general has readily dismissed the possibility that pseudo-science, scientism, or misrepresented and false scientific claims summarize the current mental health construct.

The Bible Claims to Have the Answers

Though secular science is unconvincing as an authority or a trustworthy object of faith, it is not enough for believers to reject deceptive theories. Instead, believers must be fully convinced that Christ is sufficient to address their greatest needs and the needs of those around them. It is important that a genuine

---

[319] "Sigmund Freud (1856-1939)," http://www.iep.utm.edu/freud/#H2.

[320] Satel and Lilienfeld, *Brainwashed*, 50.

[321] Such was a view and practice of the psychiatrist Benjamin Rush—whose face remains on the official emblem of the American Psychiatric Association (Lieberman, *Shrinks*, 70).

solution to people's values, mental, emotional, and behavioral issues address both nature and nurture. Scripture provides such an answer in 2 Peter 1:3: "His divine power has granted to us all things that pertain to life and godliness, through the knowledge of Him who called us to His own glory and excellence." God has given to us through the knowledge of Himself "all things" concerning (1) life (the fallen state of the world: experiences that require our mental, emotional, and behavioral reactions)[322] and (2) godliness (our personal fallen condition). To state it differently, God's grace tells believers how to be more like Christ (be restored) and enables them to respond to life's circumstances and environments in such a way that gives God glory and gives them peace. Christian counselor Ed Welch writes about 2 Peter 1:3,

> Given the degree to which God has revealed himself and ourselves, we can assume that the Bible's counsel speaks with great breadth, addressing the gamut of problems in living. It is certainly able to speak to the common problems . . . . But it also speaks to distinctly modern problems such as depression, anxiety, mania, schizophrenia and attention deficit disorder, just to name a few. . . . It doesn't offer techniques for change that look like they came out of a cookbook. But through prayerful meditation on Scripture and a willingness to

---

[322] The word *life* in this text is commonly interpreted as only referring to eternal life (e.g., John Calvin, *2 Peter*, electronic ed., Calvin's Commentaries [Albany, OR: Ages Software, 1998], 2 Peter 1:3). But there is no indication in the context that the word should be limited to eternal life. Certainly, eternal life should be included in the understanding of the word *life*, but Peter did not offer the qualifying word *eternal* to limit the word's meaning. Instead, he declares that God's divine nature provides people with all they need for all of spiritual life (temporal and eternal). In fact, verse 4 states that His precious promises enable man to escape the "corruption in the world caused by evil desires." Corrupt desires are not merely internal problems, but influential realities in the world. If God can provide all that is needed to escape eternal damnation, then it is understandable that He can also provide a spiritual escape from the corruption found in this world. Furthermore, when a person places his faith in Christ, he or she receives new life. From that point on, that person's life is in Christ (whether in this world or the one to come). So, eternal life begins at conversion. The word *life* in this text should not be limited to eternal life. Rather, Christ gives all things necessary to escape the fallen condition of the world and to remedy spiritual death.

> receive theological guidance from each other, we find that the biblical teaching on creation, the fall, and redemption provide specific, useful insight into all the issues of life.[323]

Most believers would not argue that God's Word offers hope and counsel for things that are clearly issues of salvation and godliness as the text states, yet many overlook that God addresses life itself, that is, the breadth of human experience in a fallen world. Secularists often refer to these issues as issues of nurture. Of course God provides answers to issues of nurture and nature, since He is the loving architect of life (both temporal and eternal) and the Creator of humanity. Verse four reiterates this point that God's divine nature (as observed in His precious promises) enables the believer to escape being corrupted by his or her environment. The "corruption in the world" (not only our own spiritual hearts) includes the curse of sin on creation itself as well as the common corruption of others both of which influence our lives and from which we need spiritual deliverance. In Romans 8:19-22 Paul writes,

> For I consider that the sufferings of this present time are not worth comparing with the glory that is to be revealed to us. For the creation waits with eager longing for the revealing of the sons of God. For the creation was subjected to futility, not willingly, but because of him who subjected it, in hope that the creation itself will be set free from its bondage to corruption and obtain the freedom of the glory of the children of God. For we know that the whole creation has been groaning together in the pains of childbirth until now.

This "bondage to corruption" directly affects our mindsets as we live in this world. Only a relationship with God enables us to be restored to Christ-likeness (to His glory) and escape the destructive and corrupt nature of the world we live in.

Through narratives, maxims, prophecies, metaphors, direct statements, and the incarnation, God the Father offers the

---

[323] Ed Welch, "What Is Biblical Counseling, Anyway?" *Journal of Biblical Counseling* 16, no. 1 (1997): 3.

believer His wisdom and grace. In fact, it is Christ's own character that uniquely qualifies Him to meet our needs; He has personally experienced the pain and suffering of life, while uniquely maintaining the standard of perfection that God the Father requires. The commentator Michael Green writes,

> He does not give us all we might like, but all that we need for *life and godliness* (cf. 1 Thess. 4:7f.). These gifts are enshrined in Jesus Christ himself, and in getting to know him we enjoy the power to live a holy life. But what is it that attracts a man to Jesus? His own unique (*idiā*) 'glory and excellence' (RSV). Jesus Christ calls men by his moral excellence (*aretē*) and the total impact of his Person (*doxa*).[324]

This moral excellence of Jesus stands out against the backdrop of an earthly life not marked by perfect circumstances but rather marred by misunderstanding, rejection, pain and suffering. His experiential understanding of the human condition enables him to offer empathy as well as grace. In one sense, Christ is the therapy that all of our minds need to be made whole.

Life events that are traumatic, hurtful, and stressful create needs that God's Word is fully capable of handling because it provides the sufferer with God's wisdom, comfort, and hope. When we do not approach or address these issues of life and godliness with God's wisdom, however, then we create deeper problems.

In order to approach man's mental, emotional, and behavioral struggles, we all must either view people as amoral objects and products of evolution or view them as created souls in morally relevant physical bodies. The correct anthropology and the only one that will lead to valid and helpful remedies for the mind is that he is psychosomatic, consisting of both a body

---

[324] Michael Green, *2 Peter and Jude: An Introduction and Commentary*, vol. 18, Tyndale New Testament Commentaries (Downers Grove: InterVarsity, 1987), 81–82.

and a spirit. Even the psychiatrist Peter Breggin identifies the reality of how one's worldview affects his approach to mankind:

> If we are beings rather than devices, then our most severe emotional and spiritual crises originate within ourselves, our families, and our society. Our crises can be understood as conflicts or confusion about our identities, values, and aspirations rather than as biological aberrations. And as self-determining human beings, we can work toward overcoming those feelings of helplessness generated by our past spiritual and social defeats.[325]

Though Breggin approaches mental health from a secular worldview, he still conveys the importance of having faith, and he realizes the contrast of secular models of man with true anthropology. Unfortunately, he places faith in self-reliance and foregoes the true remedy for mental illness. Yet he does identify—without using the terms *sin* and *fallen*—that mental turmoil originates from each person's own fallen human condition, the fallen condition of others, and the fallen world. Breggin concludes about many of his secular peers:

> The typical modern psychiatrist—by disposition, training, and experience—is wholly unprepared to understand anyone's psychospiritual crisis. With drugs and shock treatment, the psychiatrist instead attacks the subjective experience of the person and blunts or destroys the very capacity to be sensitive and aware. No wonder the treatment of mental patients often looks more like a war against them. It often is.[326]

Scripture, however, not only claims to have the answers to both the nature and nurture realities that shape who we are and the mental struggles that we all have, but it is completely sufficient through the true knowledge and power of God to meet humanity's greatest needs. In addition to its sufficiency, God's Word is the chief conduit that reveals His love for mankind.

---

[325] Peter Breggin, *Toxic Psychiatry*, 25.

[326] Ibid., 26. This war, which Breggin notes, will be discussed at length in the next volume.

Accepting a right anthropology requires people to accept our dual nature. Professor of medicine, Dr. Bruce Lipton explains,

> I will draw the proverbial line in the sand. On one side of the line is a world defined by neo-Darwinism, which casts the other side of the line as the "New Biology," which casts life as a cooperative journey among powerful individuals who can program themselves to create joy-filled lives. When we cross that line and truly understand the New Biology, we will no longer fractiously debate the role of nurture and nature because we will realize that the fully conscious mind trumps both nature and nurture. And I believe we will also experience as profound a paradigmatic change to humanity as when a round-world reality was introduced to a flat-world civilization.[327]

Though Lipton denies the gospel, he understands that a right view of people—as both spiritual and physical beings—is not only essential to solving the nature vs. nurture debate, but that it will correct many false beliefs currently claimed to be scientifically valid positions, the current construct of mental illness being one such theory. No matter which anthropology a person chooses, the decision to accept an authoritative source of information about mental illness will be based on faith.

Understanding the spiritual nature of our minds as created by God helps us better understand ourselves and better connect to God in whose image we are created. Failing to see and accept the dual nature of man as Scripture sets forth creates worse individual and social problems that then must also be remedied.

---

[327] Lipton, *Biology of Belief*, preface xxvii.

CONCLUSION

The construct of mental illness represents an anthropological theory mostly based upon faith rather than validated science. At its foundation, the secular construct is an extension of evolutionary thinking and the creation of the father of modern psychiatry, pharmacology, and the brain-dysfunction theory, Emil Kraepelin. Kraepelin's original construct was heavily philosophical and theoretical, resting on beliefs in materialism, determinism, and utilitarianism. Neo-Kraepelinians still hold to these same underlying beliefs, but they have managed to better disguise these philosophies with their faith in supposedly valid science. The modern version (neo-Kraepelinian or medical model) of the construct still advocates the foundational tenets that Kraepelin first proposed, but it has been revised with the addition of Spitzer's qualifiers of enduring distress/impairment and a greater belief in scientism.

The scientific process is very much a part of the current construct, but the process has not provided any scientific discovery or empirical evidence to validate Kraepelin's original theory. Instead, the faith of the modern psychiatry rests in the hope that the scientific process will one day prove the underlying theories and secular beliefs that people are merely physical byproducts of evolution and that people's moral mindsets, emotions, and behaviors are sovereignly controlled by the amoral brain and fixed genetics.

Furthermore, to hold to the current construct of mental illness is to embrace Kraepelin's theory and to accept the APA as the authority regarding the human mind, emotions, and behavior. While psychiatry continues to teach its theories as fact and to control the construct of mental illness, many — even among psychiatrists — are beginning to question the unfounded claims and assumptions by which psychiatry maintains its authority. One of the greatest issues of concern is the non-existent standard of normalcy. Though a clearly defined and established definition of normal still does not exist, hundreds of alleged deviances from this standard comprise the current construct of mental illness. This reality further exposes the current construct of mental illness to be a subjective and unreliable theory based on faith in an evolutionary anthropology and popular opinion.

To be sure, the issue of normalcy is challenging because it is a faith issue. Any theory of normalcy in regards to the immaterial mind is really an anthropological position rooted in one's theory of origin. Choosing to accept Darwin's theory is to accept the view of humanity that sees human beings as machines selected and programmed by nature without responsibility for internal or external actions, machines which can be shocked, injected, recoded, labeled even discarded when they appear to malfunction.[328] This ideology sees people as inherently good and naturally without impairment. When they become distressed or impaired, they need to be taken in for repair in attempt to restore them to a non-existent standard. Likewise, this view exalts the mechanic or the doctor who studies and attempts to fix the machine. Another choice is to view humans through the lens of the Bible which sees each person as a creation, purposefully designed by an omniscient Creator in His own image, a material being with an immaterial spirit. The former view requires faith in creation and humanity; the latter faith in the Divine. What is

---

[328] This point will be developed further in the next volume.

clear and agreed upon in both approaches is that humanity has mental problems that desperately need solutions.

Despite mainstream thought about mental illness, Christians must grasp the fact that their faith in God as Savior and Creator of their souls and bodies does not end when it comes to understanding and approaching the mind. This reality makes right theology and an intimate relationship with God essential to mental health. Likewise, such an understanding reveals and establishes what normal truly looks like, what causes mental, emotional, and behavioral struggles and what truly remedies our common mental disorder. Unlike the secular construct, however, the Bible clearly defines normalcy and answers all surrounding questions regarding issues of life and godliness.

In order to address the clear problems of the human mind, each individual's faith must rest either in the ever-changing theories of fallible men and women or in the unchanging and reliable wisdom of God. Whichever belief people choose will determine their trusted authority, their definition of normalcy, their understanding of abnormalities, and ultimately their dependence to remedy mental, emotional, and behavioral impairments.

APPENDICES

APPENDIX A – Unnatural Mindsets that Positively Change Man's Life

Philippians 4:1-13 offers us seven areas of mental discipline that come through knowing the mind of Christ (Phil. 2).

1. *We need to have the same mind in the Lord. (4:1-3)*

   "Therefore, my brothers, whom I love and long for, my joy and crown, stand firm thus in the Lord, my beloved. I entreat Euodia and I entreat Syntyche to agree in the Lord. Yes, I ask you also, true companion, help these women, who have labored side by side with me in the gospel together with Clement and the rest of my fellow workers, whose names are in the book of life."

2. *We need to have a joyful mind. (4:4-5)*

   "Rejoice in the Lord always; again I will say, rejoice. Let your reasonableness be known to everyone. The Lord is at hand."

3. *We need to have a dependent mind on God the Father. (4:6-7)*

   "Do not be anxious about anything, but in everything by prayer and supplication with thanksgiving let your requests be made known to God. And the peace of God, which surpasses all understanding, will guard your hearts and your minds in Christ Jesus."

4. *We need to have a virtuous mind. (4:8-9)*

   "Finally, brothers, whatever is true, whatever is honorable, whatever is just, whatever is pure, whatever is lovely, whatever is commendable, if there is any excellence, if there is anything worthy of praise, think about these things. What you have learned and received and heard and seen in me —

practice these things, and the God of peace will be with you."

5. *We need to have a satisfied/content mind. (4:10-12)*

    "Not that I am speaking of being in need, for I have learned in whatever situation I am to be content. I know how to be brought low, and I know how to abound. In any and every circumstance, I have learned the secret of facing plenty and hunger, abundance and need."

6. *We need to have a mind of faith set on Christ. (4:13)*

    "I can do all things through Him who strengthens me."

7. *We need to have an eternally focused mind. (4:14-20)*

    "Yet it was kind of you to share my trouble. And you Philippians yourselves know that in the beginning of the gospel, when I left Macedonia, no church entered into partnership with me in giving and receiving, except you only. Even in Thessalonica you sent me help for my needs once and again. Not that I seek the gift, but I seek the fruit that increases to your credit. I have received full payment, and more. I am well supplied, having received from Epaphroditus the gifts you sent, a fragrant offering, a sacrifice acceptable and pleasing to God. And my God will supply every need of yours according to his riches in glory in Christ Jesus. To our God and Father be glory forever and ever. Amen."

APPENDIX B – *Ways That We are Deceived*

Jeremiah 17:9 states that our spiritual hearts/minds are incurably sick and full of deception. But how do we know if we are living according to our deceptive nature or according to God's truth? We know the content of our spiritual hearts by knowing God's wisdom and allowing it to reveal our hearts. The following descriptions indicate some ways in which our spiritual hearts can be characterized by deception:

1. We believe we do not need God's grace.
   James 1:22; 1 Peter 1:13-19 – We hear God's Word (or neglect it) but remain unchanged.

2. We believe we are something we are not (pride).
   a. Romans 12:3; Galatians 6:3 – We think more highly of ourselves then we should.
   b. 1 John 1:8 – We think or say that we have no sin.
   c. 1 Corinthians 3:18-19 – We think we are wise.

3. We believe we are morally good/ religious.
   a. James 1:26 – We lack self-control.
   b. Matthew 7 – We base our righteousness on our works.

4. We believe we are above consequences
   a. Galatians 6:7 – We think we will not reap what we have sown.
   b. 1 Corinthians 6:9-10 – We change God's moral and holy laws.
   c. 1 Corinthians 15:33 – We choose immoral company.

BIBLIOGRAPHY

American Psychiatric Association. *Diagnostic and Statistical Manual of Mental Disorders: DSM-IV-TR*. Washington, DC: American Psychiatric Association, 2000.

American Psychiatric Association. *Diagnostic and Statistical Manual of Mental Disorders*. 5th ed. Washington, DC: American Psychiatric Publishing, 2013.

American Psychology Association. "ICD vs. DSM." *Monitor on Psychology* 40, no. 9 (Oct 2009): 63.

Barkley, Russell A. *ADHD and the Nature of Self-Control*. New York: Guilford, 2005.

Bentall, Richard. *Madness Explained: Psychosis and Human Nature*. New York: Penguin, 2003.

———. "Madness Explained: Why We Must Reject the Kraepelinian Paradigm and Replace It with a 'Complaint-Orientated' Approach to Understanding Mental Illness." *Medical Hypotheses* 66, no. 2 (2006): 220-33.

Boteach, Shmuel, *Moses of Oxford: A Jewish Vision of a University and Its Life*. London: Andre Deutsch Ltd, 1995.

Breggin, Peter R. *Toxic Psychiatry*. New York: St. Martin's Press, 1991.

Chan, Diana, and Lester Sireling. "'I want to be bipolar': A New Phenomenon." *Psychiatrist* 34, no. 3 (2010): 103-5.

Cherry, Kendra. "What is Humanistic Psychology?" http://psychology.about.com

"'Complaint-Orientated' Approach to Understanding Mental Illness." *Medical Hypotheses* 66, no. 2 (2006): 220-33.

Coville, Walter, Timothy Costello, and Fabian Rouke. *Abnormal Psychology: Mental Illness Types, Causes, and Treatment*. New York: Barnes and Noble, 1960.

Dispenza, Joe. *You Are the Placebo: Making Your Mind Matter*. New York: Hay House, 2014.

Doward, Jamie. "Psychiatrists under Fire in Mental Health Battle." *Guardian*, May 11, 2013. http://www.theguardian.com/society/2013/may/12/psychiatrists-under-fire-mental-health?CMP=share_btn_tw.

Eagleman, David. *The Brain: The Story of You*. New York: Pantheon Books, 2015.

Frances, Allen. *Saving Normal: An Insider's Revolt against Out-of-Control Psychiatric Diagnosis, DSM-5, Big Pharma, and the Medicalization of Ordinary Life*. New York: HarperCollins, 2013.

Green, Michael. *2 Peter and Jude: An Introduction and Commentary*. Vol. 18. Tyndale New Testament Commentaries. Downers Grove: InterVarsity, 1987.

Greenberg, Gary. *The Book of Woe: The DSM and the Unmaking of Psychiatry*. New York: Blue Rider Press, 2013.

Grossman, Dave. *On Killing: The Psychological Cost of Learning to Kill in War and Society*. Rev. ed. New York: Back Bay Books, 2009.

Hallowell, Edward M, and John J. Ratey. *Delivered from Distraction: Getting the Most out of Life with Attention Deficit Disorder*. New York: Ballantine Books, 2005.

Harris, Sam. *The End of Faith: Religion, Terror, and the Future of Reason*. New York: Norton and Company, 2005.

Hubble, Mark A., Barry L. Duncan, and Scott D. Miller. *The Heart and Soul of Change: What Works in Therapy*. Washington, DC: American Psychological Association, 1999.

Klerman, Gerald L. "The Evolution of a Scientific Nosology." From J.C. Shershow, *Schizophrenia: Science and Practice*. Cambridge, MA: Harvard University Press, 1978.

Knezev, Sasha, and Gregory Smith. *American Addict*. Torrance, CA: Pain MD Productions, 2013.

Kraepelin, Emil. *Lectures on Clinical Psychiatry*. New York: Hafner, 1968.

Kutchins, Herb, and Stuart A. Kirk. *Making Us Crazy: DSM: The Psychiatric Bible and the Creation of Mental Disorders*. New York: Free Press, 1997.

Kyziridis, Theocharis. "Notes on the History of Schizophrenia." *German Journal of Psychiatry* 8 (2005): 42–48.

Lieberman, Jeffrey A. *Shrinks: The Untold Story of Psychiatry.* New York: Little, Brown and Company, 2015.

Lipton, Bruce H. *The Biology of Belief: Unleashing the Power of Consciousness, Matter and Miracles.* New York: Hay House, 2005.

Maxmen, Jarold. *The New Psychiatrists.* New York: New American Library, 1985.

McKane, William. *Proverbs: A New Approach.* Philadelphia: Westminster, 1970.

Menninger, Karl. *Bulletin of the Menninger Clinic* 53, no. 4 (July 1989): 350-52.

Micale, Mark, and Roy Porter, eds. *Discovering the History of Psychiatry.* New York: Oxford University Press, 1994.

Mondimore, Francis Mark. *Bipolar Disorder: A Guide for Patients and Families.* 3rd ed. Baltimore: Johns Hopkins University Press, 2014.

Nikkel, Gina. "How to Fix the Broken Mental Health System: Ten Crucial Changes." *Psychiatric Times,* November 7, 2014. http://www.psychiatrictimes.com/career/how-fix-broken-mental-health-system-ten-crucial-changes#sthash.bWF2sHtk.dpu.

www.nimh.nih.gov.

Oliver, Jeffery. "The Myth of Thomas Szasz." *New Atlantis* no. 13 (Summer 2006): 68-84.

Panksepp, Jaak, ed. *Textbook of Biological Psychiatry*. New York: John Wiley and Sons, 2004.

Patel, Vikram, et. al. *Mental and Neurological Public Health: A Global Perspective*. San Diego: Academic Press, 2010.

Pert, Candace B. *Molecules of Emotion: The Science behind Mind-Body Medicine*. New York: Scribner, 1997.

Pierre, Joseph. "A Mad World." March 19, 2014. http://aeon.co/magazine/psychology/have-psychiatrists-lost-perspective-on-mental-illness/.

Popper, Karl. *Philosophy of Science: An Historical Anthology*. ed. Timothy McGrew, Marc Alsperctor-Kelly, and Fritz Allhoff. New York: Wiley and Sons, 2009.

Porter, Roy. *Madness a Brief History*. New York: Oxford University Press, 2002.

Powlison, David. "Is the Adonis Complex in Your Bible?" *Journal of Biblical Counseling* 22, no. 2 (2004): 42–58.

www.psychcentral.com.

www.psychiatry.org.

www.psychologytoday.com.

Reznek, Lawrie. *Evil or Ill?: Justifying the Insanity Defense*. New York: Routledge, 1997.

_____. *Peddling Mental Disorder: The Crisis in Modern Psychiatry*. Jefferson, NC: McFarland, 2016.

Ropper, Allan H. "Two Centuries of Neurology and Psychiatry in the *Journal.*" *New England Journal of Medicine* 367 (July 5, 2012): 58-65.

Rose, Steve, and Hilary Rose. *Alas, Poor Darwin: Arguments against Evolutionary Psychology.* London: Vintage Publishing, 2001.

Rosemond, John, and Bose Ravenel. *The Diseasing of America's Children: Exposing the ADHD Fiasco and Empowering Parents to Take Back Control.* Nashville: Thomas Nelson, 2008.

Rosenhan, David. "On Being Sane in Insane Places," *Science* 179, no. 4070 (January 19, 1973): 250-58.

www.russellbarkley.org.

Sargant, William. *Battle for the Mind: A Physiology of Conversion and Brainwashing.* New York: Harper and Row, 1971.

Satel, Sally, and Scott Lilienfeld. *Brainwashed: The Seductive Appeal of Mindless Neuroscience.* New York: Basic Books, 2013.

Scheff, Thomas J. *Being Mentally Ill: A Sociological Theory.* Chicago: Aldine, 1966.

www.sciencemuseum.org.uk.

Schwarz, Allen. "Idea of New Attention Disorder Spurs Research, and Debate." *New York Times* (April 11, 2014).

———. "Still in a Crib, Yet Being Given Antipsychotics." *New York Times* (December 10, 2015).

Scull, Andrew. *Madness in Civilization: A Cultural History of Insanity from the Bible to Freud, from the Madhouse to Modern Medicine*. Princeton, NJ: Princeton University Press, 2015.

Seife, Charles. "How Drug Company Money Is Undermining Science." *Scientific American* 307, no. 6 (December 1, 2012).

Shorter, Edward. *A History of Psychiatry: From the Era of the Asylum to the Age of the Prozac*. New York: John Wiley & Sons, 1997.

Simon, Robert, and Liza Gold, eds. *The American Psychiatric Publishing Textbook of Forensic Psychiatry*. Washington, DC: American Psychiatric Publishing, 2010.

Spiegel, Alix. "The Dictionary of Disorder: How One Man Revolutionized Psychiatry." *New Yorker* (January 3, 2005). http://www.newyorker.com/magazine/2005/01/03/the-dictionary-of-disorder.

Stip, Emmanuel. "Happy Birthday, Neuroleptics!" *European Psychiatry* 17 (2002): 115-19.

Sullivan, Harry Stack. *Interpersonal Theory of Psychiatry*. New York: W.W. Norton Company, 1953.

Szabo, Liz. "A Manmade Disaster: A Mental Health System Drowning from Neglect." *USA Today* (May 12, 2014).

Szasz, Thomas. "The Myth of Mental Illness." *American Psychologist* 15 (1960): 113-18.

———. *The Myth of Psychotherapy: Mental Healing as a Religion, Rhetoric, and Repression.* New York: Anchor Press, 1978.

———. *Psychiatry: The Science of Lies.* New York: Syracuse University Press, 2008.

Valenstein, Elliot. *Blaming the Brain: The Truth about Drugs and Mental Health.* New York: Basic Books, 1998.

Van der Kolk, Bessel. *The Body Keeps the Score: Brain, Mind, and Body in the Healing of Trauma.* New York: Penguin, 2014.

Walker, Sydney. *A Dose of Sanity: Mind, Medicine, and Misdiagnosis.* New York: John Wiley and Sons, 1996.

Watters, Ethan. *Crazy like Us: The Globalization of the American Psyche.* New York: Free Press, 2010.

Welch, Ed. "What Is Biblical Counseling, Anyway?" *Journal of Biblical Counseling* 16, no. 1 (1997): 3.

Whitaker, Robert. *Anatomy of an Epidemic: Magic Bullets, Psychiatric Drugs, and the Astonishing Rise of Mental Illness in America.* New York: Broadway Books, 2015.

Whitfield, Charles L. *The Truth about Mental Illness: Choices for Healing.* Deerfield Beach, FL: Health Communications, 2004.

www.who.int.

Wootton, Barbara. *Social Science and Social Pathology*. London: Allen & Unwin, 1968.

Wykes, Til, and Felicity Callard. "Diagnosis, Diagnosis, Diagnosis: Towards *DSM-5*." *Journal of Mental Health* 19 no. 4 (2010).

Made in the USA
Middletown, DE
14 November 2020